STRATEGIZE
TO
WIN

The New Way to Start Out, Step Up,
or Start Over in Your Career

CARLA A. HARRIS

AVERY
an imprint of Penguin Random House
New York

AVERY

an imprint of Penguin Random House LLC
penguinrandomhouse.com

First trade paperback edition 2022
Previously published in hardcover by Hudson Street Press
Copyright © 2014 by Carla A. Harris

Most Avery books are available at special quantity discounts for bulk purchase for sales promotions, premiums, fund-raising, and educational needs. Special books or book excerpts also can be created to fit specific needs. For details, write SpecialMarkets@penguinrandomhouse.com.

THE LIBRARY OF CONGRESS HAS CATALOGUED THE HARDCOVER EDITION AS FOLLOWS:

Harris, Carla A.
Strategize to win : the new way to start out, step up, or start over in your career / Carla A. Harris.
p. cm.
ISBN 9781594633058
1. Career development.   2. Vocational guidance.   3. Career changes.
4. Success in business.   I. Title.
HF5381.H149 2014 2014031571
650.1—dc23

ISBN (paperback) 9780147516541

Printed in the United States of America
1st Printing

Book design by Eve Kirch

Praise for *Strategize to Win*

"Though I'm in my fifth career (so far!), I devoured *Strategize to Win*, eager for Carla's signature pearls of leadership wisdom. As usual, she delivers a powerful message. *Strategize to Win* is the essential career handbook every young person needs starting out, and everyone else will benefit from reading regardless of age or stage of life. Carla's advice is as practical as it is precise; it's down to earth and authentic, clearly from the pen of someone who has walked the walk. You'll find something in this book to use every day."

—GLORIA FELDT, COFOUNDER AND PRESIDENT OF TAKE THE LEAD AND AUTHOR OF *NO EXCUSES: 9 WAYS WOMEN CAN CHANGE HOW WE THINK ABOUT POWER*

"Carla Harris has provided an indispensable guide to finding the career that's right for you and strategizing your way to the top. Chock-full of case studies and practical advice, it's an essential tool for professionals at any stage of their careers."

—DORIE CLARK, AUTHOR OF *REINVENTING YOU*

"Wouldn't it be great if there was an instruction manual on 'becoming a professional'? Incredibly, Carla Harris has written it. *Strategize to Win* is packed with wisdom and incisive advice. I highly recommend it to anyone, at any stage in his or her career."

—JESSICA BACAL, AUTHOR OF *MISTAKES I MADE AT WORK*

"*Strategize to Win* provides practical advice on effective techniques on getting started and getting ahead. This book should prove helpful to college students starting out in life AND seasoned professionals already established in the corporate world."

—TERRIE M. WILLIAMS, FOUNDER AND PRESIDENT OF THE TERRIE WILLIAMS AGENCY

"As a mentor to many in business I am always amazed when I ask the question, 'What is it you want to do in your career?' and the answer is most often 'I don't know.' If you have not defined what the ideal job is for you and devised a plan to get there, your chances of getting there are greatly diminished. In *Strategize to Win*, Carla Harris provides practical advice on how to look within yourself and discover the career journey that will lead you down your path to success. She also teaches you how to communicate this plan to others and to enlist their help in getting you there. I wish this book had been around when I began my career thirty years ago. It is truly a recipe for success."

—BECKY BLALOCK, AUTHOR OF *DARE*

"Everyone who strives to get ahead wants and needs mentors, but most of us lack them. *Strategize to Win* is a mentor in book form, giving you direct access to some of the finest career advice you'll ever get from one of the best mentors you could ever have."

—EARL G. GRAVES JR., PRESIDENT AND CEO, BLACK ENTERPRISE

"A highly practical guide for people in their early to mid-careers or newly transitioning to a corporate environment. The rich examples make unspoken expectations in corporate environments visible and the step-by-step instructions will be very helpful for people who are struggling to navigate their personal and professional lives in today's corporate environment."

—LAKSHMI RAMARAJAN, ASSISTANT PROFESSOR, HARVARD BUSINESS SCHOOL

CONTENTS

INTRODUCTION

When *Expect to Win* was published in 2009, we were at the beginning of a historic fiscal crisis. The real estate bubble had burst and we headed into one of the most severe downturns of consumer confidence that I have seen in my professional career, and began a period of labor unemployment not experienced since the seventies. Many people, across all industries, at all levels—entry, senior officer, exempt, nonexempt, from the boardroom to the post office—found themselves either without a job or restructured out of one, stagnating in their profession, or taking any position just to have an income. Rather than consider how a particular job might add to their skill set and prepare them for their dream job or career, many recent graduates accepted jobs to ease worries about paying off school loans or because they feared being out of the job market for too long. As a result, during my travels around the world, I have met many people who are having difficulty figuring out what career to pursue, how to make the most of the first few years of their career, and how to position themselves for success.

I have also spent time with people with five to ten years of work experience who are struggling with managing change, and are trying to figure out how to navigate the choppy waters of their careers, as their companies have downsized, they have been demoted, their job descriptions have changed, or their bosses have left or were fired. Some of these professionals are also in a quandary about why their careers haven't progressed the way that they envisioned back when they finished their academic or experiential training. I've also found that many of these professionals are struggling to read the career signs, those subtle messages that are often communicated in behavior rather than words in most corporate environments. As a result, they are puzzled about what will fulfill them professionally and personally, and how to redirect and reposition themselves and their career successfully. Further, I have talked with people who are ten to fifteen years into their jobs who always wanted a meaningful career, but rather took a job just to have one, and now, because they have "put in so many years on the job" or have family or financial obligations, they don't know how to decide what they really want to do for a career, or are afraid to take the leap to start something new.

Strategize to Win is a direct response to the people I've met and the questions they asked while I was on the road talking about *Expect to Win*. My hope for this book is that both young and mid-level professionals will find the answers and tools they need to get started in their career, to get "unstuck," to redirect and crystallize their paths, and to position themselves to manage their career through any economic cycle or any corporate political environment and continue ascending toward success!

In this book, I will define a process of deciding on a career trajectory, and more important, define a process of positioning yourself for the opportunity that you want, no matter what stage of your working life. Whatever stage we are in, we all have to reposition ourselves for new opportunities. Whether you are looking for your first job, want to move up in your company, or leave it for a competitor or an entirely new industry, you will need these tools in order to enhance or insure your success. I will also address what you must do to be successful once you land a position. Because what got you there won't be the thing that will keep you there: the skills that helped you land a position won't be the same skills that will insure your success in that role. Last, I will also identify and clarify issues that are often murky for young and mid-career professionals and help them develop the key answers they need to create strategies for reaching the level of career success to which they aspire.

STARTING OUT

CHAPTER 1

Choosing a Career in Today's Economy

"A journey of a thousand miles begins with a single step."
—Chinese philosopher Lao Tzu

Congratulations! You've just graduated or are soon to graduate from college. Or maybe you're just leaving the military. Whatever the case, you've worked hard and completed years of extensive education and training. You should be proud of yourself, what a wonderful accomplishment!

The problem is, you're asking yourself: "Now what?"

After all of those years of hard work and dedication, you find that you have no real idea of what career you would like to pursue.

Or perhaps your situation is different. You've been out of college for a few years. After graduation you accepted a job because you needed one. You had student loans and bills to pay, perhaps a family to support, or other financial obligations. But now, a few years later, you find that this job, this company, or even this career is not for you. You're frustrated, bored, and unenthusiastic. You'd like to make a move, but you have no idea what job, company, or career you are interested in. Worse, you have no clue how to begin to do anything to change it.

If any of these scenarios sounds familiar, you are not alone. Together, we are going to walk through a framework that will help you to sort out the appropriate next move in your career journey. Notice, I did not say that we are going to figure out what your entire career will look like.

Not yet.

That's too ambitious and overwhelming. We're going to start with the first step and determine the best *next* career move for you.

The End of the Ultimate Career Plan

It's true that the quest for the "ultimate career plan" was once all the rage. But in today's professional world, that kind of thinking is out-of-date. There was a time when advancing as a professional with one company, like IBM or Chase Manhattan Bank, over a twenty-five- or thirty-year period was the epitome of success. That kind of track record meant you had made it. You enjoyed the highest level of success and your financial and cultural status reflected that.

But today, aspiring to one career, with one company, doing one thing for two or three decades or more just doesn't make sense. The environment we live in is dynamic and fast-paced. Technology has massively restructured, redefined, disrupted, and in some cases even destroyed industries and businesses. In the twentieth century, it was possible for a company to maintain its leadership position over decades; but today, given the fast pace of technological innovation and the leadership life cycle in most corporations, it is difficult for one company to maintain the number one, or even number two, position in its industry for even just ten years.

In fact, it was just a short time ago that moving from one company to another was considered a negative on one's résumé. But today, success requires you to take a different approach to career planning. The new, more sensible, strategy is to consider your career in six to eight modules of five years each. And these modules could potentially be at five or six different companies. For example, you may choose to do two five-year modules with Company A in one type of role, leave to complete your third module at Company B, and then return to Company A in a more senior role. If you aspire to success and to working for a leading company in a leading industry, making changes like this is a given.

Here's why.

To remain an industry leader, a company must continually reinvent and reposition itself by making significant and consistent financial, technological, and cultural investments. The truth is, most companies just don't do that. If the company you work for isn't constantly reinventing itself to remain at the forefront of innovation in its industry, and you are determined to work for *the* industry's leading company, whatever the industry is, the leader will change over time.

Therefore, to pursue your objective, as the industry leader changes, you will have to change companies, too. Staying too long at a company, especially if you remain in the same role, will eventually begin to compromise your professional platform. That platform includes your compensation, influence, and ultimately your career success. If on the other hand, the company that you are working for does make the foregoing investments to maintain its industry leading position, then you may have an argument for working for the same company for several of the modules in your career journey. Not only is it unlikely that you will work for the same company your entire career, however, pursuing just one career is unlikely as well. It is more likely that you'll have the chance to work at several companies and pursue a number of different careers in the same or different industries over your professional life.

How Do I Decide on What I Would Really Like to Do?

Finishing college and finding yourself unsure about what professional life you want to pursue and how to pursue it is common. Further, pursuing a career, and then deciding a few years later that you want to make a change, is fairly common, too.

It's important to emphasize, particularly if you are just starting out, that there is no need to worry or feel pressured to make the exact right decision today about a career that could last thirty, forty, or even fifty years. It is pretty rare to stumble onto *the* job just out of school. Some people are lucky and have an internship they really enjoy, for example, and know from the start what they want to do. I actually was fortunate enough to fall into that category. From my very first internship at an investment bank, I knew I wanted to work on Wall Street.

Others might be driven by wanting to have a certain lifestyle and will choose a job they believe offers the salary to achieve that. Still others will finally decide upon a career through the process of elimination: trying a number of different jobs and experiences before deciding on the one to pursue.

Each of these strategies can help you to arrive at a career that you will find fulfilling and that will position you for success. You might, however, be someone who doesn't know where to start; if this is you, there is an easier, less painful way to determine what you would like to do. You will find the answers to your career questions not in knowing the job itself, but in defining the *content* of your job.

Defining the Content

Think of the content as the building blocks. Content is not a specific job or career, but rather the components that make up a job or career. While you may not know exactly what you want to do at twenty-two or even thirty-two years old, you probably know what you like to do in life in general. Consider your hobbies. What do you find interesting, intriguing, stimulating, or challenging? What are you doing when hours go by and you barely notice? What would you do even if you weren't paid for it? Asking yourself these kinds of questions is the first career move I want you to make. It will help you determine the content of your career.

This is an important exercise. No matter what stage of your career you find yourself at, you can always refer to the content you identify now for ideas and direction, as well as a reminder of your goals. It takes effort, but it's an important first step, whether you are just graduating or you have fifteen years of work experience.

In fact, if you do the tough work now of figuring out what experiences you want to have, what skills you want to acquire, what kind of people you want to interact with, or what environment you want to work in, you can set yourself up for success, experience after experience. You'll be able to make a job flow into a career, extend your success runway, and take off, ascending to the top. Keep in mind that sometimes that means taking the less popular path. No matter what path you choose, it is *your* path. This is *your* life and you are presumably going to work for a large part of it. So it is in your best interest to position yourself for success by pursuing something that you like or that is consistent with *your* life plan.

By developing the content for your career now, you can save yourself a lot of heartache, angst, and worry in ten years, when you realize that you need to change your job or career and doing so is a lot harder. As we go down the road of life, we tend to become more risk averse because we have financial and/or family obligations. Many of us become complacent, and even though we may not be happy, we stay in jobs because we fear change or think it's too late to do something new. Doing the content work now will make it easier for you to chart your moves throughout your career, because you will know to pursue the jobs that contain the components that you enjoy, are good at, want to learn, or are motivated to do.

Start with three blank sheets of paper.

At the top of page one write: *If money were no object, how would I spend my days? What would my job look like?* This is your content.

On the top of the second sheet write: *What jobs have this content?*

And, on the top of the third sheet of paper, write: *What skills, experiences, or education do I need in order to be eligible for these types of positions?*

If Money Were No Object

Page one is designed to help you think through how you would like to spend your professional days if money were no object. Do you like sports, do you like entertainment? If you like entertainment as an industry, do you like music, film, theater, video, art? Do you want to perform, or do you want to manage other artists? Do you like working with things that involve numbers? Do you think you would like finance, or computers? Do you like figuring out how things work? Do you like science? If so, do you like biology, physiology, astronomy, or chemistry? These are some of the questions that you might ask yourself when trying to discern what you like.

Then you might ask yourself questions such as:

- Do I like working alone or in teams?
- Do I like problem solving or executing?
- Do I like building processes or developing solutions?
- Do I like things that require me to use my analytical or quantitative skills or am I more partial toward doing things that require me to use my writing and/or creative skills?
- Do I like convincing people to do things?
- Do I think that I would enjoy selling products or services that I like or would I simply like the challenge of trying to convince people to do/buy something, and what I'm trying to convince them to do/buy doesn't matter?
- Do I want to do something where I am directly involved in helping people every day?
- Do I like figuring out puzzles?
- Do I think I would like spending my time in an open environment where everyone works together to solve problems?
- Do I like environments where everyone has their own assignment and we later come together to see how all of the pieces fit?
- Do I like working on things in a high-energy, fast-paced environment, under pressure?
- Do I prefer my assignments planned ahead of time or do I find the idea of new assignments each day exciting?
- Do I like to travel and want to get on a plane or train several days a week?

- Would I prefer to work in the same location each day with no travel?
- Do I like working with people of different ethnicities, backgrounds, etc.? Do I like working in an environment where I will be required to use different languages?

While considering these questions, I challenge you to think about things in your life that have always interested you, hobbies and other activities that you currently do or enjoy. For example, did you like playing sports as a student? Did you continue to pursue that sport in college? Are you committed to a life of constant practicing? Are you good enough to pursue that sport professionally? Then, dig a little further: Did you also like working on a team with others to pursue a goal? Would you like to coach others in the sport? Would you consider being a physical therapist treating professional athletes, or an orthopedist focusing on high school, collegiate, semiprofessional or professional athletes? Do you have strong communication and/ or writing skills? Would you like writing or reporting on the sport? Could you report on sports on television or radio?

Alternatively, what was your best subject in high school? If it was art, for example, would you enjoy working for a museum, being an art critic, writing about art for a newspaper or magazine, or being an artist?

Especially early in your career, it is important that you focus more on content than a specific job. Why? Particularly in challenging economic times, the content of the job will be far more important than the specific job itself. In a difficult economy, when most companies typically cut back on personnel and try to conserve costs, the reality is that your dream job may not be available. If, however, you take an alternative position that allows you to acquire the basic skills necessary for your dream job, when the economic environment improves you will be well positioned to sell yourself into the job you really want. For example, suppose you are interested in working in ad sales at a magazine, but no matter how hard you try, those jobs remain few and far between, and the only people even getting interviews are the most experienced sales execs. You have very little, if any, experience.

So instead, you accept a job telemarketing and selling home security services over the phone. Not your dream position, but you'll develop skills in getting prospective clients on the phone, keeping them engaged, and making sales. Later, you can use that experience to convince a hiring manager that your phone skills will translate to face-to-face sales for a product that you believe in, in this case the magazine. Now you can approach your dream job with not only aspiration but real sales experience.

It is understandable that many recent college grads focus on just getting a job, any job, figuring they can find their dream job once they have a foot in the door. *I strongly advise you against taking this approach.* It's important to give careful consideration to the content of any job you take, even an entry-level one, to make sure it allows you the opportunity to develop the skills and experience you will need to land the job you really want.

During the financial crisis that began in 2008, I saw so many young professionals accepting whatever job they could find. They were afraid of the looming recession. I saw seasoned professionals who were laid off quickly jumping to any position without thought to how it would fit in with their future and overall career goals. As a result, when the economy began to improve a few years later, those same people had difficulty landing the jobs they really wanted. They could not explain how the jobs they took prepared them for a better position or fit into their overall career plan.

Content matters. It should be one of the key factors you focus on when deciding on a job or a career. Even if your primary reason for accepting a position is the money it will pay you, there should be something else about the job that's consistent with your aspirations or the skills that you'd like to acquire. No prospective employer likes to hear that you took a position for the money. Focus on content first and you will be much better off.

There are usually several different jobs that can offer you the content you want. This is good news, because it expands your opportunities. Let's assume the content of your dream job includes selling things. You like convincing people to make a decision to buy something. That means you could sell clothes, insurance, stocks, pharmaceuticals, consulting services, shoes, engineering services, industrial products, commercial ads, Internet ads, and the list goes on.

Ask yourself what kinds of things you might enjoy selling. What are your favorite products? What brands do you believe in? What would be challenging for you to sell, what would be a breeze? The content is the same, selling is selling. The question is which product is going to inspire, challenge, or excite you every day to sell it?

So many MBA candidates tell me they want to work in investment banking and mergers and acquisitions because they want to acquire valuation skills. But there are several jobs within the financial services industry that would expose them to valuation analysis. For example, as a sell side equity research analyst, the primary skill they would hone is the ability to value a company and make a comparative analysis of companies in an industry. In credit research, they would learn how to value a company and assess its comparative creditworthiness. As a private equity investment banker, they have to learn to value companies in order to make purchase or selling recommendations. While the overall job description and key success factors are markedly different for each role, each position would teach an MBA graduate the desired content: how to do valuation analysis. By focusing on the content and not just a specific job in mergers and acquisitions, these individuals could markedly expand the kinds of opportunities that are available to them.

It's also important to note that, as you consider the content of the career you desire, you shouldn't limit yourself to interests based on only the things that you have done before. Consider things that are intriguing or interesting to you for whatever reason, in the spirit of "you don't know what you don't know." If it interests you, consider including it on your Content Page. You may not discover why it intrigues you until later. Have you always been fascinated by finance? Do you like the entertainment industry? If so, what part of the entertainment industry—recording arts, performance management, arts facility management, movies, Broadway theater, radio, videography?

The goal is to fill your Content Page with as many interests as possible. This will allow you to identify several jobs or careers that will position you to be successful. Your ultimate professional success is all about how you position yourself, and that starts with landing a position that engages you because you like doing it, are interested in it, and you want to learn it because you like the content.

Now, let's turn to the second piece of paper in our exercise: what jobs have this type of content?

What Jobs Have This Content?

First, let me applaud you. Completing the Content Page is no easy task.

Admitting we don't *really* know what we want to do is hard to do. If we're younger, in college or graduate school, it can be difficult to admit. Society expects that we are in school pursuing *something* that will lead to a successful career. It is so easy to go with the flow and pursue jobs and opportunities that are popular or considered prestigious by the people who matter to you—peers and especially parents who have sacrificed to put you through college. You go along knowing, deep down, that even though you may have earned the credential, degree, or certificate, you still don't have a clue about what to do next. Or worse, let's say you have decided that after three years of law school you really don't want to be a lawyer! As we continue to get older, we avoid the truth even more assiduously. We put our heads down and plow forward, rarely stopping to allow ourselves to ponder the question for very long.

When I was in college, all of the top economics students were flocking to Wall Street analyst positions, two-year internships with one of the top management consulting firms, or law school. While there were a few people going into brand management or on to other graduate programs, very few had the courage to consider becoming an entrepreneur or starting out in the mail room of an entertainment or artist management company to get a foot in the door somewhere they could pursue a personal passion and use their degree at the same time. My classmates who weren't econ majors were also trying to pursue these types of jobs, even if they had an interest or passion to teach high school or become a book editor. Many of my colleagues and friends took at least ten years after college to figure out what they really wanted to do, losing valuable time that they have could have used to ascend in careers in which they were *really* interested.

So now you have done the hard work of thinking about the answers to questions like "How would I like to spend my day?" "What type of job content would have me excited about getting out of bed to go to work?" "What activities would I be happy doing for free?" Now you are ready to start considering the kind of jobs that contain that content—our Jobs Page. For example, if you like math or working with numbers, you might consider pursuing accounting or working in a commercial bank. If you like writing, you may think about working at a newspaper, writing columns for a magazine, or becoming a book editor.

In positioning yourself for success, however, I want to challenge you to go beyond the careers that you already know have the right content and consider opportunities that might not be within your current purview. Completing your Jobs Page also involves learning about jobs and careers that you currently know nothing about. This will require research. Choosing the right job or career means spending time talking to people and networking. People often miss opportunities that they might find professionally fulfilling simply because they don't know they exist. Maximizing your options—and therefore your success—means understanding those options.

Begin by putting aside at least one week out of every month (or the equivalent of 100 hours), to do nothing but research and talking to people about what they do. If you're already working, I don't mean that you take a week off to pursue this activity. I am suggesting that over the course of one month, you find at least 100 hours to talk to others about what they do. You can do this by asking people out for coffee, lunch, or breakfast, or even when you are meeting new people through informal get-togethers with your friends. When you meet people, ask them questions about what preparation or experience they needed to do their jobs; what some of the key benefits or drawbacks of their specific job or career might be; or how they got to where they are. If you are not working, then you should be spending at least three days out of every week researching various opportunities and meeting with people. Use your network to get introduced to people who may be pursuing careers that you are interested in. For example, use your alumni network or make an appointment to talk with a former professor about their previous students and the jobs that they accepted after graduation. Ask if he or she would introduce you to a former student. Take the opportunity to have more in-depth discussions with your professors about the types of jobs they had before becoming educators or what type of work they considered. This will help to give you ideas about ways to leverage the intellectual content they have, and that you have now acquired through your studies.

As you research, make notes on your Jobs Page and keep track of all of the jobs that have content that you are interested in. It is important to do this research so that you can make an informed decision about what roles you want to pursue, instead of longing to do something and assuming you won't be able to.

In today's environment, it's easy to do this kind of research because there is so much information on the Internet about people and what they do. If you don't know anyone personally that you can network with, look to find information on the Internet that describes the opportunity that you are interested in. Read newspaper or magazine articles, blogs, or other sources about someone who does something similar to what you have interest in.

I find that often people don't pursue things that have always interested them because for some reason they don't believe they can find a job that they will enjoy and that will allow them to support themselves. Yet most of the time they have never done the research to determine if that were really true. I recently had a conversation with Gregory, a twenty-year-old college sophomore who was unsure what he wanted to do with his professional life. He did know that he wanted a career that would allow him to help his parents and siblings and the family that he hoped to build. During the course of our conversation, Gregory mentioned that he had been a terrific high school basketball player, but he constantly got hurt because he did not know how to properly care for his injuries. He spent most of his time on the team sidelined.

As a result, Gregory thought he might like to help high school athletes avoid spending as much time injured as he had. He also mentioned that he liked tinkering on his smartphone and was intrigued by technology. Gregory had never had a conversation with anyone about his interests in sports medicine and technology. He just assumed that there was no way for him to combine them. He also knew that his family was going to have a hard time helping him get through college to pursue one degree in four years, so he did not see how he would have enough money for the extra year necessary to complete another degree.

I suggested he could pair his interest in sports medicine with his interest in technology by considering biology, physiology, or industrial or mechanical engineering as areas of discipline in college. These majors would enable him to experience different types of courses within one discipline and have a wide range of career opportunities. Ultimately, he could work as an orthopedist; an engineer using technology to create orthopedic medical devices; or he might want to make mechanical limbs for veterans, athletes, and others. In just one conversation, Gregory went from articulating an interest in something to having five different career options!

Having as many conversations as possible with as many people you can about your career aspirations will help you expand your ideas and bring to light options you may never have considered. These valuable choices will help you craft a career over time that is built upon the content that excites and motivates you. Further, it will help you to reposition yourself later, if and when you decide you want to change or start a new career.

In addition to speaking to people about jobs that have the content you're seeking, you can also start to crystallize what you want to do by spending time in an environment that interests you. For example, you can volunteer, or even take a job or internship that may not have the exact content that you want but puts you in the right environment and gives you exposure to jobs that may fulfill you.

You will be surprised by what you learn during this exercise. Let's suppose that your Jobs Page analysis led you to conclude that you want to work in a hospital environment. While you're not sure if you want to be a doctor or a nurse, you've determined from your Content Page that you like science and quantitative analysis, and that you want to help people each day. Why not then spend three to six months volunteering in a hospital? This would give you the opportunity to learn about the different jobs available there and would offer you the chance to speak to the various professionals you might encounter, in the elevator or over coffee.

If you don't have time to volunteer, you could offer to take someone you know in that field to lunch. Even your own or a friend's doctor would be a good candidate. Talk to them about the kind of people that typically work and do well in a hospital environment. Ask questions like: What are some of the key factors for a successful career in this field? In addition to patient care, what types of jobs are available? What relationships are necessary to be successful in their role? Who do they have to interact with in order to be successful? This last question might lead you to other people in the hospital or industry that you could also speak to.

Continuing with our hospital example, let's say you notice that there is a hospital president whose job it is to make sure that the hospital not only services patients but that it also runs like a business. This person may or may not be a medical professional, but has most likely been trained in business or has held a series of management or operational jobs in medical institutions. They might have been the director of purchasing, the director of personnel, or the director of logistics at previous jobs. Combined, these previous positions make them the ideal candidate to efficiently run a hospital, making sure it has the resources it needs to attract top medical experts, the facilities necessary for an esteemed medical institution, and all with outstanding margins and profitability.

They might tell you that what sets their hospital apart from others is the exceptional clinical research lab and introduce you to the head of their research facility. You might then get the chance to meet with or observe the lab's clinical researchers to understand what they do and what they like about their work.

The president's job, the researcher's job, and the many other jobs you are likely to learn about while researching and networking would all fulfill your criteria of working in a hospital environment and contributing to the welfare of people every day. And you could do this without ever having to draw one ounce of blood! But had you not spent time talking with people who actually work there, you may never have known about these types of opportunities.

What Skills, Experiences, or Education Do I Need to Be Eligible for These Types of Positions?

Once you have compiled a list of the types of jobs that would have the content that interests you, it is time to turn to page three: "What skills, experiences, or education do I need in order to be eligible for these types of positions?"

Remember, your ability to obtain a role depends on your academic and experiential credentials and how well you sell yourself and your capabilities. It might surprise you to know that I believe there are very few jobs where your prerequisite experience is the dominant factor in the decision to hire you. In short, the job search process is similar to a sales transaction. The key to successfully getting through an interview and acquiring a job is actually highly dependent upon your understanding of what the buyer (the interviewer) is really buying and how well you sell it (your background and experience) to them.

When preparing for an interview, identify the key factors and skills necessary to make you successful in the job. Then consider what you have done in your past, academically or experientially, that would convince the interviewer that you are the right person for this role. In some situations, there will be minimum academic prerequisites necessary for you to be considered, but in other situations your experience as well as your ability to tell your story will determine if you get the position.

For example, if you want to be a doctor, you have to complete undergraduate and medical school. If you want to be a lawyer, you'll need to get a law degree and pass the bar. On the other hand, if you want a job in pharmaceutical sales, the requirements may be less definitive. The posting for the position may state that the company "prefers" someone who has X amount of sales experience.

Let's consider the key success factors for a job like this.

To be an outstanding pharmaceutical salesperson you must be:

- a self-starter—can work independently, taking on projects with little supervision and direction
- a relationship builder—able to meet people (doctors) and form connections quickly
- a good listener—can figure out quickly what matters most to others and therefore what arguments you need in order to complete a sale
- a quick study—can learn about products and services and get up to speed on new information quickly
- results-oriented—always have the end goal in mind (the sale)
- creative thinker—always thinking about what tactics to use and how to convince potential buyers to make the purchase
- driven—motivated to exceed your sales goals
- personable—can work well with others, people enjoy having you around

In your interview, use what you learned in preparing for the meeting to articulate your understanding of the key success factors for the position and offer evidence that in your previous experience, whether it was a sales position or not, you delivered on all of these factors and how you will be able to do so in this new position.

Certainly, if you do have previous sales experience and demonstrated success in that role, it will be an added benefit. But more important, if you have *not* had prior experience it should not be an insurmountable challenge or a deterrent to going after the job you want. You simply have to present the experience you do have in the right way.

When I landed my first Wall Street internship, the only corporate job on my résumé was my experience working at McDonald's. I was sixteen years old and still in high school when I became a crew member for the Golden Arches. That, a summer at a law firm, and two years of college-level economics was all the "experience" I had. As I sat in that interview chair and began to talk with the recruiter, I told him about how I was made Crewmember of the Month while still on my ninety-day start probation. And that I was also named Crew Chief while I was still in high school. I explained that I frequently won informal prizes for suggesting ideas about increasing sales, and I almost always had the highest-grossing cash register on the nights I worked.

While none of this experience was technically Wall Street related, it communicated important ideas to the recruiter. He (the buyer) was looking to hire (buy) someone who was respected by their peers and clients, had a commercial orientation, and could penetrate client thought to make the sale. In addition, my grades, activities, and honors at Harvard communicated that I was a fast learner.

The company could teach me about stocks and bonds, but what the buyer was *really* buying were the other success factors necessary to shine on Wall Street: self-motivation; the ability to connect with others, gain their respect, and figure out what they wanted; and an appetite for winning.

On your page three, your Skills, Experiences, Education Page, write down the credentials of people who currently have the jobs from page two that pique your interest.

Take a look at a company that is in the business in which you're interested. You can go online to find its annual report, available on most company Web sites. Review the list of the company's officers and/or its board of directors. There are generally biographies of each member of the senior management and the board of directors. Read each bio carefully, looking for any commonality in experiences, schools, and so forth. Also, compare management biographies across companies for a particular position, again to discern if there are any common paths for professionals who ascend to those positions.

For example, if you want to be a chief marketing officer (CMO) in a large corporation, look at the bios of several CMOs across different industry verticals to see if there is one common path or even similar majors that they pursued in school. In the case of marketing officers, you will see that some CMOs had traditional brand management roots; some came from media organizations, while others have backgrounds in public relations and promotions. The obvious conclusion here is that there is no one clear path to being a chief marketing officer. Assuming that you have the core competencies that are necessary and could sell your previous experiences into the role, you could obtain such a position coming from various disciplines.

If you don't see a commonality among the people who have the positions you think you might want, then you have a good indication that your ability to land the position will be more dependent on how and with whom you network, and how well you sell your story. Alternatively, if you look at the biographies of chief financial officers (CFOs) across various industries, you will find invariably that each has had previous experience in finance (usually as a treasurer, comptroller, or director of finance roles) before ascending to CFO. You could then conclude that you would only be an attractive candidate for a CFO position if you had previous experience in one of those areas, no matter what your academic training might have been. We'll spend more time in Chapter 2 discussing how to make yourself attractive for that next opportunity.

What About Being an Entrepreneur?

If you are considering whether you should forgo the corporate world to strike out on your own, there are a few things that you should seriously consider before making this move. First, determine if your product or service is something that satisfies a real market need or is something that will create demand, like the social media industry.

Let's consider the social media products available to us today. First, who would have thought ten years ago that we would all be interested in reading about and looking at what our friends and acquaintances are doing, thinking, and creating at any given moment? Who would have thought that it would be commonplace to go into a restaurant and snap a picture of your food and then send it to people you think might be interested?

Second, if you have a product or service, then ask yourself, Who else offers a similar product? Why is yours different? How will you convince customers that yours is better, cheaper, or preferable? How much money will it take to get to market? How will you market your product or service? How will you attract customers? Who will provide the capital for the business? Do you have enough money to get started or to sustain your business for at least a year if no one buys your product or service? How many people will you need to successfully run your business, as you cannot run it alone? If it is a business where you are the one providing the service and you make all the decisions, then your growth is going to be capped by what you as one person can physically and mentally do. Do you know how to develop a solid business plan? If not, do you know someone who can do that for you? Do you know how to present to prospective investors or banks?

As you can see, there's a lot to consider if you are going to start your own business. It is a decision that should be made very carefully. You should not conclude that you would be better off doing so just because you are having a hard time finding employment. If it is your dream to start your own business, then I strongly suggest that you acquire experience working for someone else first. That will allow you to learn about and hone skills and resources that are needed to actually start, maintain, and grow a business—and you can do it all on someone else's dime.

Let's say, for example, that you think you want to start a software company. Seek to find a position with one of the larger, more established software companies so that you can really understand how to organize and run a research and product development department. Then perhaps move to a smaller company to learn how they attract and pitch to investors, how they manage cash, what systems they use for hiring people, and how they manage their cash burn.

Or, maybe you would like to run a nonprofit. Seek out an opportunity working for an established one, so that you can learn the challenges of hiring and retaining a strong development staff and how to manage legislative relationships that could impact policies (that could in turn affect your nonprofit or the people that you wish to serve).

The more experience you have around the product or service that you want to offer the market as an entrepreneur, the more credibility you will have with prospective investors and customers once you head out on your own.

◄ *Carla's Pearls* ►

1. It is not uncommon to find yourself graduating or leaving the military, or even be several years into working, and not know what you want to do. In today's world, most professionals will have an opportunity to have several careers over thirty, forty, or even fifty years. Don't panic. Just get started!

2. Content is the most important thing to focus on when you are looking for employment, either early in your career or mid-career. It is the foundation of your job and career plan. Take the time to define it for yourself.

3. There are three questions that you must ask yourself to position yourself for a job that you want: 1) What kind of content do I want in my job? 2) What kind of jobs have this content? 3) What skills, experiences, or education do I need in order to be attractive for a job with this content?

4. When you go on interviews, know what the buyer is buying, and then sell your understanding of that, as well as your skills and experience, and why you are the best candidate for the job.

5. If you want to be an entrepreneur, you should seek to get experience and education in the area you're interested in by working for someone else first. Make sure that you have a strong plan and adequate financial and personnel resources before you start your business.

CHAPTER 2

Making Yourself Attractive for That Career Opportunity

"If you spot an opportunity . . . and are really excited by it, throw yourself into it with everything you have got. Be ambitious."
—Sir Richard Branson

Now that you have an idea of what you would like to do, how do you get access to the opportunity? How do you get the interview? In today's professional environment, many companies are using online applications as a way to assess candidates who are interested in employment. Although companies visit college campuses and career fairs to find potential candidates, the Internet offers an efficient way for a company to "see" as many candidates as possible and then narrow the list, inviting only those they are most interested in for a face-to-face interview. Many companies are also using telephone interviews as a way of further screening the candidate pool before inviting them for an in-person meeting.

I have had many job applicants tell me that they can't get an interview because they can't differentiate themselves from the hundreds or thousands of other people who are applying online for the same job. I would agree that if the Internet is the only method you are using to land an interview, then it might indeed be difficult to make your résumé stand out. I am a big fan of augmenting your online process with the old-fashioned approach of writing a strong cover letter and résumé, and then mailing it via overnight delivery to the hiring manager. While professionals may procrastinate in opening the snail mail that comes to their office, most people open an overnight delivery immediately. As a result, your candidacy will get noticed for consideration.

Another strategy to help you get that important face-to-face interview is to spend time researching the company, its officers, board of directors, or in the case of a nonprofit its key funders and supporters. You may discover that someone you know works at the company, is on the board, or is a major funder of the organization. Don't hesitate to aggressively use your network and ask that person to forward your résumé to the hiring manager or to someone at the company who can do so. Few things will make a hiring manager take notice of a candidate's résumé faster than a recommendation from a senior manager or current employee of the company.

When you are seeking an interview for a new opportunity, your network is an important tool. When you are in college or grad school, companies often come to your campus to interview prospective candidates or participate in job fairs in your area that specifically target undergraduate and graduate students. However, once you have graduated, your ability to land an interview depends upon your résumé being noticed among a pool of applicants. Your network of contacts, and the contacts' ability to use their political and social capital to get your résumé noticed by a hiring manager or requesting you be granted an interview is a key to your success.

Your network can be particularly helpful in landing what's referred to as an "informational interview." This is an opportunity to visit a company, meet a few people, and ask questions and acquire information about the areas of the business that you might be interested in. The intended purpose of an informational interview is for you to familiarize yourself with a company to decide if you want to pursue formal interviewing with that company, for a specific job or department.

While an informational interview is not supposed to be evaluative, don't be fooled into thinking that you are not being evaluated. You are being evaluated, make no mistake! Anytime someone is meeting you for the first time, they are indeed evaluating you. It is human nature. They may not be taking notes while you're talking, but they are still forming a perception about you that could help or hurt your chances of getting a formal interview and eventually a job.

If the person you meet for your informational interview decides they like you, they'll subsequently recommend to the hiring manager that they should conduct a full interview. The informational interview is a valuable tool, but I want to offer a word of caution. It can be risky. If an informational interview doesn't go well, perhaps because you didn't ask the right questions, or the interviewer didn't feel that you had done the right research, demonstrated your intellect, or even if the person you spoke with was having a bad day, then the perception of you could be a negative one. In that case, it's not likely the person you met would recommend you to the hiring manager or that you would be granted a formal interview. That negative experience could even affect your application if you decided to pursue a position at some point in the future.

I believe that you should only use the informational interview as a tool for getting a formal interview when you already know a few people in the organization and feel very prepared to handle yourself successfully—as if you were in a real interview. Even though the meeting's purpose is to gather information, you must be prepared to be evaluated and show your best self.

Success in the Interview

While every interview is different, there are ten common questions most interviewers ask. Undoubtedly there will be other questions that may be specific to the role that you are seeking. However, the following are basic questions almost any interviewer, in any industry, will ask you, particularly in the first round of interviews.

In addition to researching the company and the position you are applying for, spending time thinking about and preparing yourself to answer these questions will give you a good foundation for any interview and go a long way to making you an attractive candidate.

1. Tell me about yourself.
2. Why are you interested in this position?
3. Why are you interested in our company?
4. What makes you different from other candidates that we might see?
5. Why do you think that you can do this job when you haven't had direct experience in this area?
6. Why should we hire you?
7. Can you tell me about a mistake that you made?
8. What are your strengths?
9. What are your weaknesses?
10. Do you have any questions for me?

Do I Need Another Educational Credential?

In addition to the top questions interviewers ask, one of the other topics that often came up as I toured the country talking about my first book, *Expect to Win*, was education. I met many professionals looking to make a job or career change. I can't count the times people said, "I am going back to school, so that I can _____." Anyone who knows me knows I AM A BIG FAN OF EDUCATION. I am a woman with two Harvard degrees and seven honorary doctorates, which I cherish.

The reason this statement gives me pause, however, is that people automatically believe that additional education will be a panacea. It seems that people assume that the first step to making a career change is going back to school. They rarely consider that they may already be qualified for the opportunity they are seeking, without the financial and opportunity cost associated with getting another degree. Sometimes more education is necessary and is the only way you can advance—but not always. Before you commit to becoming a student again, make sure you know *why* you are doing it and how you are going to use your new degree, certificate, or other credentials.

Let's say you aspire to become a lawyer. Then, it's true, you *have* to go to law school and pass the bar exam. In financial services, and in investment banking in particular, you could start your career with a company and move your way up the ladder, or come to the firm as a lawyer or experienced industry hire. But the smoothest path into the investment banking business is an MBA. Most investment bankers (not all, but most) have MBAs from one of the top graduate business programs. If you plan to work in an information technology position, you'll generally only be considered if you have a Microsoft or programming language certification.

Suppose, however, you are interested in working in corporate philanthropy and your previous experience is as a mortgage restructurer. You have an undergraduate degree in English, a reputation for demonstrating excellent judgment in your work, great analytical skills, and are very involved in your community. You don't necessarily need to pursue a master's in philanthropy or social work to qualify for the job.

The first question to ask yourself is derived from the factors we discussed in Chapter 1: What is the buyer really buying? In other words, what would an interviewer look for in a potential candidate for this kind of job? What are the key success factors for this job? To be successful in corporate philanthropy you have to be astute, have the ability to conduct due diligence on nonprofit organizations, and have good judgment about their needs and ability to apply contributions effectively. You must possess strong relationship and analytical skills, and have an affinity or passion for nonprofit work and the community.

In your previous experience as a mortgage restructurer, you would have developed relationship-building skills. Your success in that position would have depended on your ability to speak to people and get them to trust you; due diligence skills and ability to analyze situations and your client's ability to pay; and ability to apply good judgment in structuring a new payment plan. Further, your position as a trustee or as head of your church's outreach ministry, combined with a good, sound argument about why you are interested in the job, can make you as competitive as someone with a degree in philanthropy and no previous work experience.

When deciding if you need more credentials or a certain level of experience for a new role or career, spend time (I recommend at least three months) speaking to as many people as possible who are doing what you would like to do. Study their journey. Do they all have a college degree? Is it a prerequisite for that position? Do they all have master's or professional degreès? Did everyone study the same subject field? Have they all worked in the same positions and followed the same path before they obtained their current job? As we discussed in Chapter 1, your goal is to determine if there is a widely accepted route that most professionals in that industry take, a certain degree or other credential that they get, or, rather, if certain skills are required to work in the industry.

If there is a prescribed route, such as obtaining a certain credential like law school and the bar exam for lawyers, or medical school and internships for doctors, then you'll have to pursue those graduate programs. Or if you must become a marketing assistant and a marketing manager before becoming head of marketing (or follow some other predetermined route), then you'll have to do that. If, on the other hand, there is no particular credential or path required, then look carefully at the skills and experiences that are valued in the role, determine which ones you have already developed, and start acquiring the others that will make you attractive for the job you want.

You'll also want to consider not only the job you are interviewing for, but the one after it, and even the next role as well. Since few of us stay in the same job for our entire careers, the best time to assess the chances for advancement is when you are initially interviewing to join the company. We'll discuss this more in Chapter 3.

If you have basic professional skills—marketing, exposure to finance or financial principles, presentation skills, organizational and people management—from five or more years of experience in the working world, then you already have applicable, salable basic skills for almost any industry. The key is to understand what the interviewer is looking for. In other words, you have to determine what the key success factors for the position are and then connect the dots for the interviewer by convincing them that you are the right person for the role.

Here's an example of how you might connect the dots.

Vincent was a military officer who managed several platoons over the course of his military career. He worked on a telecommunications mission and was responsible for setting up communication towers and other facilities while soldiers were deployed. He was also responsible for training new soldiers and was assigned to give extra training to those who had a particularly hard time passing through some of the early stages after enlisting. After he left the military, he started looking for an opportunity where he would have direct contact with customers or clients, and ideally, be able to help former military professionals.

Vincent heard about a job working in an organization that helped to place former military professionals in corporate environments. The job description stated that there was a "preference" for applicants with a Master of Social Work (MSW) and at least two years of experience working as a social worker. While Vincent did not have a MSW or specific experience as a social worker, he did have other skills that would be key to success in the role. The posting also listed the following as crucial to success in the role: 1) have an understanding of the customer (military personnel); 2) be able to build and connect easily in relationships and be a good listener; 3) have excellent problem-solving skills and be resourceful; 4) have strong sales skills (as he might have to sell prospective companies on potential candidates); and 5) have an understanding of available training resources in the marketplace.

Let's break it down and compare Vincent's experience with the job's requirements:

1. **"have an understanding of the customer"**

   As a military officer, Vincent worked closely with military personnel. He certainly understood the culture and had personal experience with typical issues and challenges transitioning from military life to civilian life.

2. **"be able to build and connect easily in relationships and be a good listener"**

   Vincent could point to his ability to motivate and train soldiers who were underperforming as evidence for his strong relationship and listening skills.

3. **"have excellent problem-solving skills and be resourceful"**

   Vincent had no exposure to telecommunications before he joined the military, but he became so fluent that he was assigned to a leadership role in a telecommunications post, and once there effectively dealt with the challenges of deploying telecommunication stations with insufficient equipment and solving problems in real time under pressure.

4. **"have strong sales skills"**

   In his role with the military, Vincent had to "sell" the soldiers he trained on their own ability and on staying in the military. By the time they were assigned to Vincent, many of them were ready to give up and did not believe that they could have a successful career. He never lost a soldier from the training program and many went on to become successful officers.

When preparing for the interview, the primary thing Vincent would have to focus on would be job requirement number 5: **"have an understanding of available training resources in the marketplace."** Vincent clearly had the other prerequisite skills and could connect the dots between his previous experience and their relevance to the job's demands, and would need to articulate this to the interviewer in a clear, cogent, and compelling way. However, he would have to convincingly *sell* the interviewer on his ability to quickly learn and understand all of the resources that were available.

Because he had no previous experience in the industry,

Vincent would have to learn about the various resources to which he might need to refer clients. Since most of that information was publicly available, he would simply need to do the research and be able to recount the information with confidence in the interview.

It is also important to note that even though the job posting specified a "preference" or even a "requirement" for certain skills that Vincent didn't have, he should apply for the position anyway. Just because a posting articulates something as a prerequisite, if you have most of the credentials specified, there could be something else about your résumé that a prospective employer might find intriguing enough to invite you for an interview or at least grant you a phone screening. Never count yourself out!

Like Vincent, many of us have skills and experiences that are applicable to a myriad of opportunities. The difficulty in successfully mastering an interview and landing the job you want is not a lack of experience, but rather your inability to recognize the skills you already have and craft a story around those experiences. Your story has to showcase your strengths and connect this portfolio of skills and experiences to what the interviewer is looking for—what the buyer is really buying.

Your Can Do, Your Will Do, and Your Fit

Most companies will conduct at least three rounds of interviews. During that process you could easily meet ten to twenty people before you are offered the position. Remember, in any interview, the company or the organization is assessing three important things: *Your Can Do, Your Will Do,* and *Your Fit.* All of the questions you are asked will be designed to address these broad categories.

Your Can Do determines if you have the intelligence, credentials, and experience to do the job. Interviewers will get a preliminary assessment of Your Can Do from your résumé. If someone calls you for an initial phone or face-to-face interview, you can assume they have already decided that you have the basic credentials to do the job. This does not mean they have decided you are the right person for the position, or even that you have all of the prerequisites they are looking for, but you have a basic background consistent with professionals currently in the job.

When you initially sit down with an interviewer (and sometimes in the second round of meetings as well), Your Can Do skills are assessed. They will try to figure out if you have what it takes to do the job by asking you some of the questions we talked about above. They may also test your knowledge and skills further by asking job-specific questions. For example, suppose you are interviewing for a job with a strategy consulting firm. As part of the interview, it would not be uncommon for them to give you a case study to solve. One of the key things the buyer is buying is your ability to problem solve. A case study will assess how you go about dissecting and solving a problem. Often, it is not about whether you come up with the correct answer to the problem, but rather how you go about analyzing it and the process you articulate to get to your solution.

If you are interviewing for an investment banking position, you may be asked to calculate the weighted average cost of capital, or you may be asked to value a company in a particular industry. Alternatively, if you are interviewing for a job in equity sales, the interviewer might ask, "What is your favorite stock and why?" If you are trying to land a marketing position, you might get a question about the fundamentals of marketing, like, "What are the 4 Ps or the 4 Cs of marketing?" (The four Ps: *price, product, promotion, place*; the four Cs: *customer, communication, cost, convenience*.)

Each of these questions is designed to help the interviewer determine if you have the basic skills and understanding to do the job.

Your Will Do is about understanding what motivates you, your tenacity, and your willingness to persevere and be resourceful. The interviewer is trying to understand if you are a self-starter; have initiative; are self-motivated to do a great job—or if you are selectively motivated; in other words, have to be coaxed, praised, and cajoled to move things forward. Your answers help the interviewer decide if you have the qualities and personality to be successful in a certain position. In assessing Your Will Do, interviewers typically want to see that you have good judgment and are always motivated to produce an excellent work product, whether the project is considered important or mundane. Interviewers may ask you about your previous work experiences, challenges that you've had in your current or previous positions, or how you went about executing a specific project or role highlighted on your résumé. Consider beforehand the message you want to communicate when answering this category of question.

In my personal experience, when I know the interviewer is assessing my Will Do, I focus on communicating these messages:

1. I always deliver the work product.
2. I am resourceful, and if I don't know how to do the project or answer the question, I can use my skills to find out what I need to know to deliver.
3. I treat all projects with importance, both small and large.
4. I know how to prioritize.
5. I never disappoint.

I try to address these messages in my answers to *any* of the questions I am asked, but especially those that fall under the Your Will Do umbrella. Of course, you want to work them in in a way that they make sense. You always want to make sure that you are answering the question that is asked; you don't ever want to sound like you are not answering a question. But the more often you can get these messages across the better.

Your Fit is about understanding whether you will fit in at the company. Now the interviewer is thinking about the company's culture. He or she is assessing if you have the same demeanor as other employees, and if it appears your personality and work style will easily integrate with other members of the team.

Your Fit is the most subjective of all of the three categories because it is almost wholly dependent upon the interviewer's personal judgment about who you are and if you will integrate well with the way *they* see their environment. You see, there are two very important measures of subjectivity in assessing Your Fit. The first is based on the connection you make with the individual interviewer. In short, it's about how they see you. As human beings, we tend to see people through our own lens of experiences, background, and individual personality.

The second is based on the way that particular interviewer sees their own organizational environment. This, too, is subject to their own view and experience with the organization. Interviewer A may have a somewhat reserved personality and therefore may view an organization's environment as very aggressive, necessitating a new person to work extremely hard to integrate themselves into the company. That is how they view *their* experience. But, interviewer B, who works for the same company but has an extroverted personality, may describe that same company's culture as collegial and easy for a new person to navigate, particularly if the prospective candidate is a self-starter.

The key to selling Your Fit, first and most important, is to be authentically you. What you bring to the table is your personal competitive advantage. No one else can be you. Second, you have to articulate how you read the culture and why you think you could easily integrate into the team. While your assessment of the culture may or may not be congruent with the interviewer's, you will have presented a cogent argument for your views and why you should be a part of the organization.

Selling Your Story

Over the course of my career, I have interviewed thousands of people: undergraduates, graduate students, prospective lateral hires, and seasoned professionals. One of the key differentials between the candidates at various levels of experience is how they *tell* and *sell* their stories.

Telling and selling your story is one of the most important components to successfully interviewing for any position. Yet it is one of the things that candidates most often fail to do well. As a result, it is among the principal reasons why people don't succeed at positioning themselves for an opportunity.

Whether you are just starting out or have been working for several years and making a change, typically, the first question asked in most interviews is "Tell me about yourself." In this question you have the perfect opportunity to *sell* the interviewer on those attributes that they're seeking to buy. Here you have the chance to lay the foundation and send the message that you are the best person for the job. Unfortunately though, I find this is the principal place where people torpedo the interview— before they've barely even gotten started.

In telling your story, you should be prepared with the following questions in mind:

1. What is the buyer really buying in trying to acquire a candidate? What are the key success factors for the job?

2. In telling my story, where I am going to start? Am I going back to childhood, is that relevant? Should I talk about where I am from? Should I start at college and move forward?

3. How am I going to integrate the key success factors into the messages that I communicate about who I am?

Let's take a look at how you might tell your story in two different scenarios. Background: You are interviewing for a position on a pharmaceutical sales team for a new drug the company hopes will be a blockbuster product. In scenario one, you have just graduated from college. In scenario two, you have five years of retail sales experience at a major department store. As the recent college graduate, it's okay to reference high school, because those experiences are only a few years old and likely relevant to your story. Otherwise, I would not recommend telling high school stories; it makes it seem as if you haven't had much going on since you left. If you have been out of college for a while, it is okay to reference college, particularly if your college experience was integral to your realization about what you wanted to do with your early career or if the experience is relevant to why you want to pursue that particular job. No matter what your level of experience, ask yourself: What is the buyer really buying? What are the key success factors for this position?

To be successful in pharmaceutical sales, you must have strong communication skills and be able to articulate a marketing message in a compelling way. You must understand the product, which means you must be a quick study, especially if you don't have previous experience selling this product. You must be a good listener and be able to discern what characteristics or facts about the product are important to the customer. For example, do they care about how fast the drug works, its side effects, or the price per dose? You must demonstrate perseverance and tenacity because you may have to approach the customer several times before they decide to purchase or agree to try the product. You must also be goal-oriented, driven to achieve objectives, and perhaps even have a competitive spirit.

You come in dressed in your best interview attire, sit down, and the interviewer says, "Susan, thanks for coming to see us today. Why don't we get started? Tell me a little bit about you."

Scenario #1

Susan: "Thanks Tom. I appreciate the chance to talk with you today. I would be delighted to tell you a bit about me. I recently graduated from ABC University with a degree in English. I am originally from ABC State and chose that university because I wanted a program with a strong English or Communications program.

"Many of my high school mentors told me it was important to have strong communication skills no matter what career I chose, because every career requires us to have the ability to effectively communicate a message or idea, or to sell a product or service in a compelling manner. My experience at the university has been terrific. I have done very well academically, excelling in all of my classes and making the Dean's List several semesters. I have also been very involved in the drama club and debate team, and was elected a member of student government.

"Over the course of my four years at school, I have thought about various career paths and successfully obtained several internships, as you will see on my résumé. One summer, I worked as a retail sales clerk at J. Crew and during that time I also volunteered at a hospital. In my second summer, I took classes to improve my GPA, and also had a part-time job in a pharmacy within the university health services. Then, last summer I worked for a financial services firm in their sales and trading department.

"What I've learned from my academic experience and internships is that I really like selling. I like telling a story and motivating someone to take an action, to buy my idea or a product. I have also learned that I am very good at it and have been fortunate enough to be invited back to work at all of the organizations I worked or interned with."

Let's assume that you are the interviewer. What did you learn about Susan? What did she sell to you? You now know Susan is:

- Driven and motivated (she has excelled academically and has done well in a discipline that you care about, as the interviewer).
- A strategic thinker (she gave you a cogent argument about why she chose ABC University: to pursue communication skills).
- Well liked by her peers (she has been chosen or voted in to represent students on student government) and can easily form and build relationships.
- A fast learner and has a track record of doing well in professional environments and has sales skills (she received offers to return to all of her previous positions, even internships in which she had a short period of time to excel).
- Familiar with some of the customers that she might have to approach (she has volunteered in a hospital environment).

By answering just one question, Susan let the interviewer know they need not be worried that this position would be her first full-time experience. She "sold" the interviewer on the many attributes that they are interested in buying. She not only articulated each one of the key qualities, but she gave credible evidence to support each assertion that she had those skills. Susan has already given enough of a credible argument to answer the interviewer's Can Do questions and supported the perception created from a review of her résumé.

The "tell me about yourself" question is very broad, and in many cases is used as an icebreaker for the interview. If they have not prepared ahead of time, it gives the interviewer an opportunity to scan your résumé while you talk. It also gives them a chance to assess your judgment by listening to how you choose to answer. This question is one of the most important of the entire interview. It gives you an opportunity to set up your story and focus on what *you* want to sell the interviewer. Don't take this question for granted or brush it off as merely an informal icebreaker. This is an opportunity to position yourself to win the interview.

In scenario #2, Susan has five years of retail sales experience at a high-end retailer and is now seeking the position on the pharmaceutical sales team.

Scenario #2

Susan: "Thanks for the opportunity to speak with you today. I am currently working as a retail sales supervisor at ABC Company, and I have several years of sales experience. I am a graduate of ABC University, where I majored in English and developed strong communication skills, knowing they would be important to have no matter what career I chose.

"While on campus, I was very involved in student life. My most significant extracurricular experiences were on the debate team and in student government, where I was elected to several different positions. It was during those experiences and my summer internships in retail sales and financial services on the sales and trading floor of XYZ Company that I realized that I really enjoyed sales.

"I liked the idea of developing a script about a product or service, and communicating that script in a way that motivated someone to take action to buy. I also realized that I am a fast learner because during the internship in sales and trading I had to quickly learn the products and concepts so that I could communicate effectively with my team and external clients.

"I received a full-time offer at the end of that internship, but I chose instead to accept a job with ABC Company. It was a new and emerging brand, and I wanted to be in on the ground floor helping to build the product. I hoped to have an even greater impact on the company's success than I might have had in the financial services environment. It has been a terrific experience. I've learned a lot and done well, as I was promoted during my five years with the company.

"One of the other experiences I had while in college, however, was my summer as a volunteer at a hospital. I really liked the environment and found it easy to build relationships with the doctors. Given all the changes that are happening in the health care environment, I think there is an exciting sales challenge for the pharmaceutical companies. One's ability to build impactful and successful relationships with doctors and patients is going to be one of the most important contributors to success. I believe that I have the skills to do that successfully and I am interested in that kind of challenge at this stage of my career, and that is why I wanted to have this conversation with you."

As the interviewer, you learned that Susan:

- Has direct sales experience, with demonstrated success (she has been promoted at her current employer and received a job offer at the end of her summer internship in sales).

- Has strong communication skills (she studied communications and she has experience debating, which could serve her well in developing alternative sales perspectives with customers).
- Can build relationships (she was elected to student government positions).
- Is a fast learner (she picked up financial services concepts quickly, even though she had no previous experience in the sector).
- Understands what the job entails and presented the interviewer with a strong argument about why she is interested in it. She sold the following skills to the interviewer in answering the very first question: strong selling skills, strategic thinking, relationship building, results oriented, goal oriented, and the ability to learn quickly.

I would argue that Susan has successfully set herself up to win the rest of the interview. All she needs to do to position herself for success is to continue to reiterate these points in the answers that she gives to the remaining questions.

While these were two very different scenarios, in each Susan adequately used her experience to convince the buyer she could offer what they were buying. In scenario #1, while she had no "professional" experience, Susan used her studies and internship experience to articulate that she had the qualities necessary for success in the position and offered credible evidence in support of her claims. And in scenario #2, Susan used her experience in one industry and connected the dots for the interviewer showing how that experience easily translated to another.

Experience Isn't Everything

There are very few jobs where your prior experience is the dominant factor in your ability to successfully land an interview and get the job. Many job descriptions will ask for candidates with previous experience in a similar position. But let's be clear: in many cases that experience is a *preferred* qualification, not mandatory.

Sure, companies would prefer to hire someone who doesn't need training, particularly for a supervisory position—someone who can come in and immediately add value to the environment. If you can sell yourself in an interview, however, relaying that you are a self-starter, quick learner, and have a track record of successfully doing things for the first time, then you have a competitive shot at winning an opportunity with no previous work experience in that industry. You must make a compelling argument that you have *most* of the skills consistent with the key success factors of the job.

Now, let's continue on with how to position yourself for success by reviewing answers to some of the other basic questions you will be asked in those first interviews. As you progress toward getting the job, remember, you want to craft your answers to each question so that you sell that you have at least one of the important attributes for the job.

Why Are You Interested in This Position?

This is your opportunity to demonstrate that you understand what the position is, how it fits into the company, its strategy, and why it makes sense for you to have this role at this stage of your career. This is also your chance to show that you have done your homework on the company and have a genuine interest in being a part of the team. Your answer should speak to how you became interested in the functional expertise required for the job (in the above case, how you became interested in sales).

Why Are You Interested in Our Company?

In answering this question, you want to demonstrate that you know something about the company. You want to communicate to the interviewer that you are aware of the company's strengths, its strategy and outlook, and how the management views its employees. If the company is particularly proud of the way that it promotes and develops its people, be sure to mention that as a point of interest. If the company is a leader in many or all of its competitive markets, then you want to communicate your desire to be a part of a company that is focused on being a market leader. You should comment on information that is publicly available about the company as well as your perception of the company's strengths.

What Are Your Strengths?

Interestingly enough, this is a question that many people fail to answer in a way that is consistent with their sales pitch. When you are answering this question, your strengths should dovetail with the characteristics of what the buyer is really buying (which should align with your pitch, too). Each of us has many strengths and things that we are good at, but the ones that you should emphasize when you are interviewing are those that are consistent with the key success factors of the job for which you are interviewing.

For example, I have very strong quantitative, analytical, organizational, and critical thinking skills. I am also very creative, a good writer, strong communicator, a relationship builder, and results oriented. If I am interviewing for an investment banking job, I will articulate my strengths as being strong quantitatively and analytically and focus on my relationship-building skills. If I were focused on a marketing job, I would define my strengths as my creative and communications skills.

In each of these cases, I focused on those strengths that are consistent with what the buyer is really buying. I would not define my creative and communications skill as key strengths to the interviewer in the finance interview. While those are appreciated, they are not the predominant skills that would be valued in that role.

What Makes You Different from Other Candidates That We Might See?

This question also gives you an opportunity to sell your qualifications. You cannot possibly compare yourself to other candidates because you do not know who they are. The way to answer this question is to state: "While I cannot speak to the qualifications and characteristics of the other candidates, I can tell you that my skills, intellect, and experience give me the ability to add tremendous value in this role. I am a quick learner, a team player, have strong listening skills, can discern the product qualities that are important to the customer, and I believe that I will be able to positively affect sales. I have a strong history of sales experience and easily build relationships. I believe that I will be a compelling member of the team and will help the company achieve its sales and relationship objectives."

The key to answering this question is to not get lured into comparing yourself to other candidates. This is a clear runway for you to focus on why *you* are the best person for the opportunity. You should focus on the unique set of experiences that have prepared you for this opportunity. You don't want to answer with generalizations like, "I am smart," "I attended a great school and had great training," or "I work really hard," because presumably any candidate could give these answers.

Instead, you want to use those attributes that are valued in the role and personalize them, e.g., "I can discern the product qualities that are important to the customer," "I have had first-hand experience with those issues that the customer would be concerned with," or "My specific experience with _____ is directly applicable to what it takes to be successful in this role."

Why Do You Think That You Can Do This Job When You Haven't Had Direct Experience in This Area?

This question is a great opportunity for you to connect the dots for the interviewer by correlating your previous experience with the key success factors for the position. You should present the argument that you want them to articulate to others who might ultimately be involved in the hiring decision.

Using Susan, let's look at how you might answer this question. Remember, she does not have any previous direct sales experience in the pharmaceutical industry. The script would go something like this: "Even though I have not had direct sales experience in the pharmaceutical industry, I have had experience selling products during my summer internship in retail sales. I know that it is important to understand the product—in fact to be an expert on it—and to be able to articulate the product's key strengths in a compelling way.

"I learned in my previous experiences that it is important to really listen to the customer to discern what they care about and what, therefore, should be the point of emphasis in the sale. I have all of these skills and successfully deployed them in my last role, often as the highest-grossing salesperson for a given day or month. I have the ability to form relationships easily, which is key to making recurring sales, and I am a fast learner and am therefore confident that I will be able to get up to speed quickly on the key products that we want to bring to market."

Why Should We Hire You?

This question allows you to convince the interviewer that Your Fit with the company is right. If you've been able to convince the interviewer that Your CAN DO and Your WILL DO will be assets for the job, then you should answer this question by aligning your characteristics with the company attributes that you have uncovered in your research.

For example, if the company you are applying to prides itself on developing its people, emphasizes teamwork, and is very focused on execution, your answer should focus on those attributes: "I believe you should hire me because I have the skills and experiences that will allow me to add value in a very short period of time and quickly become a very effective member of the sales team. In addition, I believe that I will easily fit in with the firm's culture of teamwork and excellence in execution, as I have historically been very successful in working in groups and integrating myself quickly, as evidenced by job offers following my internships. I also believe wholeheartedly in sharing information and developing others around me and welcome others' offers to invest in me."

Can You Tell Me About a Mistake That You Made?

Many people fail to prepare for this question before they begin an interview and therefore don't answer it properly. When an interviewer asks you this question, he or she is trying to: 1) assess your judgment (what story you will choose to tell);

2) understand what lessons you've learned; and 3) determine how you recovered from the mistake. None of us is perfect. If you are alive, you have made mistakes. The answer you give for this question should send the message that you are thoughtful, reflective, have good judgment, and are not prone to repeating mistakes.

For example, when I was interviewing for a job on Wall Street and was asked this question, I gave an example of a scenario from early in my career. One of my bosses asked me to complete an assignment. While I wasn't quite sure what he was asking me to do, I decided that I should not ask for further clarification because I thought he expected me to figure it out. I was afraid that asking a lot of questions about the assignment would show that I was not very smart.

The assignment was due in five days. Luckily for me, I turned it in in four days, only to find out that it was completely wrong! I had misunderstood his directive, gathered the wrong information, processed the data in the wrong way, and given him results that were useless to him. The boss made a big, loud deal about my error. In his ranting and raving, I understood what he really wanted. I left the meeting and proceeded to stay up all night to remedy my mistake, and was able to turn in most of what he wanted the next day. Luckily, all was not completely lost.

The lesson that I learned? Don't ever walk away from someone giving you an assignment without a complete understanding of what they are asking you to do. It does not diminish your talents to ask questions. In fact, by asking questions you create a perception that you intend to deliver on the assignment because you want to make sure that you fully understand what is being asked of you. It's also a good habit to repeat back what you think you heard them say, so that both of you understand that YOU are clear on the assignment that is being asked of you.

What Are Your Weaknesses?

This question is fraught with opportunities to sink an interview. You should never answer this question with weaknesses that are consistent with the key success factors of the job that you are trying to obtain. For example, if you are interviewing for a grant-writing job for a nonprofit or as an editor with a publishing house, you should not say that one of your weaknesses is your writing skills or your ability to write in a succinct manner. If you are interviewing for a finance job, please do not say that your quantitative skills are strong but your analytical skills are weak. Believe it or not, people actually do this!

When asked this question, I articulate some skill that I am currently working to improve that has nothing to do with the job I am interviewing for. For example, I am currently working to improve my golf game and I am currently working to free up extra time to write. The question is "What is your weakness?" which means any weakness is fair game to discuss. You don't have to point out a weakness that is related to work. If the interviewer really pushes you to give a work-related example, then you can say, "I tend to spend extra time at the margin, going over and over an assignment, when I have already determined that it is right. I could be using that time to move on to something else. I am working on this problem and am much better than I used to be, but I still do it." It would also be appropriate for you to comment, perhaps, on being a perfectionist. Now, be careful with the "perfectionist" answer because a lot of people use it and the interviewer could think that you are being trite. Be prepared to give several examples of your "perfectionism," as this answer might motivate the interviewer to probe deeper about your weaknesses. No matter what, you never want to say that you are weak regarding time management, people management, prioritizing tasks, or patience.

Do You Have Any Questions for Me?

When an interviewer asks you this question, it is very important that you have an answer. Many candidates make the mistake of saying that they have no questions at the end of an interview. What this does is communicate to the interviewer that you are so nervous that you just want to get it over with; you are unprepared for the question; or that you are not really interested in working for the company.

If you have done your homework on the company and prepared for the questions asked of you, here are two of my favorite questions to ask at the end of the meeting: 1) Can you please give me the profile of someone who does really well at the company? 2) Can you give me the profile of someone who does *not* do well at the company?

The answers to these questions will give you important insights into the company's culture and will help you decide if you have the attributes, demeanor, and skills to fit in and do well. The interviewer is likely to share adjectives that are associated with success for the job and in the company, or they may describe one of the organization's superstars. This is important information for you, particularly if you decide to accept a role with the company. It will give you an idea of what you must do to create that same perception about you. Furthermore, the answer to the second question of someone who does not fit in will give you a good idea of the behaviors you should avoid so you don't set yourself up for failure.

Other questions you might want to ask when the interview concludes:

1. How did you make the decision to join this company?
2. What were the three most important questions that you asked of yourself when you made that decision,

and how would those questions be different if you were asking them today?

3. What are the company's two biggest challenges over the next twelve to twenty-four months?

4. What is the biggest investment that the company will undertake in the next twelve months?

5. Who or what is the biggest competitive threat to the company?

It is important that you have questions ready about information that would be helpful to you in either making a decision about joining that company or that might be important to your success in that particular role. If the interviewer gives you an opportunity, never leave the interview without asking at least two questions.

◄ *Carla's Pearls* ►

1. People automatically assume that in order to change jobs or careers they need additional education. That is not always the case.

2. Many of us have skills and experiences that are applicable to a myriad of opportunities. To successfully master an interview, you have to recognize the skills you already have and craft a story that showcases your strengths and connects your skills and experiences to what the interviewer is looking for.

3. *Your Can Do* determines if you have the intelligence, credentials, and experience to do the job. *Your Will Do* is about understanding what motivates you, your tenacity, and your willingness to persevere and to be resourceful. *Your Fit* is about understanding whether

or not you will "fit in" with the culture of the company.

4. Telling and selling your story is one of the most important components to successfully interviewing for any position. Prepare well for the "Tell me about yourself" question; it's your opportunity to show that you have done your research about the company and assure the interviewer that you can handle the job.

5. Many job descriptions will ask for candidates with previous experience in a similar position, but in most cases that experience is a *preferred* qualification, not mandatory.

CHAPTER 3

Positioning Yourself for Success

The Essential Skills and Exposure You Must Get

> *"You were born to win, but to be the winner you were born to be you must plan to win and prepare to win. Then and only then can you legitimately expect to win."*
>
> —Zig Ziglar

I can't count the number of people who have told me they took a job with a company thinking, "Once I get in, I can work my way around to getting the position of responsibility and authority that I really want." But despite performing very well, many have been sorely disappointed.

The fact is, the position they took "just to get a foot in the door" was not on a trajectory to a higher-profile revenue-generating role (often referred to as a line position).

All companies have a path that leads to the most senior-level positions in the organization. The path can be formal (e.g., all the leaders of a particular auto company come from the finance department, or every C-suite-level officer in a certain consumer products company has had responsibility for brand management of a revitalized brand). Or the path can be informal, where it is generally understood that people who rise to the top in an organization have had a particular experience set (for example, at least one international assignment).

Not understanding an organization's precedents may leave you frustrated when you try to make a move. Assuming that you have the ability to do the job, your disappointment will only be a function of the organization's inability "to see" someone in your position in the job you want because this kind of transfer hasn't taken place in the past.

Where You Enter Influences Where You End Up

Before you join an organization, it's important to study the environment and the people who work in it. Learn how the senior people have been chosen for their positions. These days it is easy to obtain this information by going to the company's Web site and looking at the bios of the senior leadership team, or by doing an Internet search on specific individuals to learn more about their backgrounds. Did everyone with a senior role "grow up" in the company, meaning that they started in an entry-level position and moved up over ten to fifteen years working there? Or does the company have a history of hiring people—their senior executives in particular—from the outside? Is there precedent for someone in operations moving to a line or revenue-producing assignment or from the line moving to back-office operations? Have people who worked in the treasurer's office or in accounts payable moved over to managing a consumer brand? Is there evidence that someone in an administrative position moved to a project management team where there is revenue or profit responsibility, or to a staff position working directly for the CEO, CFO, or COO? Has a certified nursing assistant been promoted to a nursing position after they finished their collegiate nursing requirements or were all the nurses recruited as nurses into the hospital versus internal promotions?

If it's important to you to earn an integral position, higher pay, or more authority in an organization, understanding what has happened in the past (your company's precedent) will help you determine what opportunities will be available. If your organization does not have a history of moving professionals from one area of the company to another, then your educational credentials and intellectual or experiential capability won't matter. Getting the opportunity to pursue the position you want simply won't happen because the organization has no precedent for the move.

The best time to assess what paths to upward mobility are in line with the position you want is when you are interviewing to join the company. If you didn't do this before accepting a company's offer, then you should try to find out how people move within the company as soon as possible after joining, or most certainly before you decide to move within the company.

If you are interviewing with someone who is senior to you, when you get to the chance to ask questions, inquire about their path up through the company. The following questions will help give you the insight you need to determine how the company promotes people:

- Does the company have a history of promoting from within the ranks?
- Have many senior executives come from outside the company?
- What is the precedent for people outside the department joining the team?
- When people in this department change roles, do they take other roles within the department or do they move around the company?

- I am trying to understand how people grow and move within the company. Can you give me a few examples?

For example, you may in the process of asking these questions learn that people generally do not go from one part of the company to another, or that there is no history of people moving from administrative roles to revenue-producing roles. Or perhaps all of the organization's senior people have had previous revenue-producing roles. Then, if you want to move into a senior position, you should seriously consider whether you want to accept an offer in a non-revenue-generating role.

Precedent gives you clear information about what the company values the most. In the previous example, I am not saying that non-revenue-generating roles aren't valued, but rather that a particular organization might view revenue-producing roles as important prerequisites to senior positions. In that scenario, your inability to move to a more senior position has nothing to do with your ability—your Can Do, your Will Do, or Your Fit (as we discussed in Chapter 2)—but it does have everything to do with the company's precedents. In the previous example, it is clear that all the senior positions have been filled with people who had revenue-generating roles. While there are exceptions to every rule, you should not accept the job thinking that YOU are going to be the exception.

Consider Ted. He took a job at a company right after receiving his MBA from one of the best business schools in the country. It was a tough market environment and Ted could not find a position where he wanted, in the strategic finance area of the company—the team responsible for identifying and executing the organization's strategic purchases. Ted thought if he took a job in accounting, he could move to strategic finance after a few years. In theory, his thinking made sense: the accounting department worked closely with strategic finance to calculate the cost of capital for transactions and transfer capital at the close of purchases.

Everyone who worked in strategic finance was either hired into the department after they received their MBA, and over time moved up in the department; transferred into the group from a manager-level position in one of the company's three key businesses; or were hired from a competitor. Those who came from the outside had the same role at their old company.

Three years after starting off in the accounting group, Ted eagerly applied for an open position in strategic finance. To his surprise, a candidate from a competitor was hired instead. The outside candidate was perceived to be more of a strategic thinker because he had experience doing similar work. It did not matter that Ted was providing finance support to the company's transactions and was intimately familiar with them, as well as with the company's strategy and even the people on the team. He had even graduated from the same school as many of the strategic finance employees. Still, because of his support function in accounting, Ted was not seen as a "transactions guy." In fact, the department had never hired anyone from the accounting team.

Take a very close look at the companies and industries you are interested in, and understand how they hire and promote people in various departments before you accept a position. Every company has a history of hiring and you need to know what it is. If people are only hired in from certain departments or promoted with certain experience, it is important for you to know that before you take a job in that area, especially if you have a different background.

If you cannot find information on the Internet about the series of roles that someone has had that led to their current position, then you can also get this information by talking to various people at the company, particularly when you are interviewing. You can ask every one of your interviewers, "Can you tell me about your history at the company?" or "What were your previous two or three roles at the company?"

On Wall Street, you will rarely, if ever, find someone from strategic planning or finance and administration moving into a role as an investment banker. In consulting, you won't find a researcher moving into a role as a strategic consultant. You won't see someone who works in logistics or purchasing at a consumer products company moving into brand management, just like you won't see someone who has been working in finance at an entertainment company get an opportunity to be a producer of a new show at that organization. Or someone who is in graphic design at a public relations agency move into an account executive role.

Again, I want to emphasize this has nothing to do with your capability or your capacity to do a job. Instead, it is about the lens the interviewer or the company is looking through when they view potential candidates for a position. If you are trying to enter an area of the company from a department where no one has ever come before, the interviewer is apt to be biased against your capability. He or she will be trying to assess your Can Do through a lens of skepticism, as well as considering the implications of such an internal transfer and what it might mean for others who might want to take the same path.

Ultimately, the interviewer might decide against you as a candidate, not because you aren't capable of doing the job, but because they are worried about how they will manage future candidates who want to do the same thing.

The Past Predicts the Future

If a company has a precedent for how people enter certain areas of the company, it will stand until a leader or other influential person in the company or department decides to break it or new leadership takes over. Generally, an organization will only see the new possibility when someone in a leadership capacity steps up and spends their professional capital to create, clarify, and execute the new vision. When there is a change of leadership in an organization or department, the message that "there is a new sheriff in town" is sent to the company, setting the stage to do things differently. Other times, a company can decide that it wants to shift its culture to one that promotes from within without changing management. Human resources might communicate a more open policy toward job mobility within the organization, which will help create an opportunity to break historical precedent. Or you can step outside a company precedent if one powerful leader decides to spend their political and social capital on YOU, because he or she feels strongly that they want you on their team and they are willing to exercise their power to make it happen. They may not be breaking precedent forevermore, but in this instance, because you are the important part of the equation, they will ignore the company's norm.

This does not happen every day and you should not go into an organization thinking you will be able to have this happen to you. This is not to say that it can't be done. It can, and you may be the first to do it in your organization. But recognize that forging a new path is rare and takes considerable performance and political currency, especially in a formal, corporate entity with a long history.

You'll have to assess your standing in the organization, your reputation for performance, and most important the strength of your relationships with sponsors and other supporters, because it will take someone else's political and relationship capital to break organizational precedence. Your ability to be the exception to the rule of mobility will be heavily dependent upon the sponsor you have in the organization and the extent of their power and political capital within the organization. You also have to recognize that if this happens to you, your performance in the role will be highly scrutinized, as there will be people who won't agree with or like the idea.

You must be ready to harness all of your intellectual, relationship, and experiential capital to excel early on in your new role. To continue to ascend in the organization, you'll have to leverage the momentum of your new position. If you fail to perform or people perceive that you're not doing everything possible to succeed, you will more than likely find yourself quickly replaced. Further, it will take you a long time to regain the support of your old sponsor and you will likely find attracting any new sponsors very difficult.

Front Office, Back Office, and Staff Roles

The term "front office" or "line position" comes from the manufacturing industry, where working on the assembly line was deemed an important position. If an employee was in charge of supervising a manufacturing "line" they were considered influential in a company.

Today, when someone uses the term line or front office, it connotes someone working in a revenue-generating role or in a capacity that is consistent with how the company makes money. It describes someone who is generally in direct contact with clients or customers, or in a role that directly impacts the customers or their buying behavior.

If you are a nurse, doctor, or someone who provides direct patient care at a hospital, you are considered to be in a front-office role. If you are working in a bookstore as the head of a specific department with responsibility for generating that department's sales, you have a front-office job. If you are working in a construction company and overseeing a group of professionals responsible for developing a commercial property, you are on the line because you are participating in an activity that directly impacts the company's revenues. If you are an investment professional working in a private equity firm, you are considered to be in a front-office role—your actions directly contribute to the company's ability to generate revenue.

A "back-office" or "nonline" position is one that *supports* the company's efforts to generate revenue. For example, most jobs in human resources, diversity and inclusion, finance, administration, technology, and operations are considered back-office roles because they do not directly touch the end customer. Yet these are vital roles because the company could not offer goods and services to customers without them. These areas have their own systems of horizontal and vertical mobility, compensation, and sometimes titles.

Don't be fooled by the nomenclature of "back office" vs. "front office" with respect to the importance or influence positions these areas might have. Each company and organization has its own culture and value system. For example, in some companies, human resources is truly a support for the business units or revenue-generating departments and is not a role that would lead to running the company. But in other companies, human resources is one of the organization's most powerful departments and senior positions in HR could very well lead to a chief executive officer role.

When you are entering a company, spend time researching and understanding the culture and the various paths of mobility. Some companies have companywide training programs that allow employees to rotate between back-office and front-office positions. If your company has these types of rotational programs you may very well have the mobility to move between front and back office, but it is important that you understand whether that's a possibility before you make a decision about your role. Doing so will help you position yourself for maximizing your success. We'll discuss this in greater detail later in the chapter.

A "staff" position is usually a management position that does not directly touch the customer, but manages a group of people or the entire company. Just as the president of the United States has a chief of staff who manages his office, his meetings, the interviews he does, and the appearances he makes, an individual with a staff role within a company often has a similar function. A staff position usually reports to the most senior people in the department or company; these jobs generally have strategic planning, personnel management, financial analysis, and other high-level content.

Many of today's CEOs retain an office of the chairman or an office of the president, made up of several professionals who report directly to them and manage the company's day-to-day affairs as well as interactions with its board of directors. These staff roles are usually short-term (one to three years) rotational positions reserved for professionals with strong track records of performance in the company. These prestigious assignments are generally characterized by high pressure and impact. When you work in these departments, you are involved with assignments that are of strategic importance and often confidential in nature. Therefore, to be considered, high-level performance, as well as a reputation for being mature and prudent, are a must. If you are fortunate enough to position yourself in one of these roles AND you do a stellar job during your assignment, you will be able to choose your next assignment and enjoy an upward trajectory in the organization.

Rotational Programs

Over the last decade, many companies have started offering rotational programs for entry-level employees. These programs are designed to give you an opportunity to explore a number of different areas within a company before you decide what role and/or career path to pursue. Some of these programs are designed to have you rotate within a specific division and others have you move throughout the entire firm.

In one particular commercial bank's eighteen-month rotational program, participants move throughout the company working in investment banking, sales and trading, the credit card division, human resources, international affairs, and operations. Conversely, a typical investment bank's rotational program is designed to have candidates move within sales and trading, capital markets, research, and investment banking over a twelve-month period. At the end, the candidate is asked to choose three areas where they would be interested in working. There is no guarantee that the candidate will get a position in one of their three choices, but typically this is the goal.

If you are the candidate, your ability to land one of your three choices will depend on the specified areas also choosing you! Therefore, it is very important that if you have an opportunity to enter one of these rotational programs, you do not view your assignments as "tryouts" for the group. In other words, you shouldn't approach the position as if you are there to just get exposure to the group to see if you like it. Whether or not it is an area of the company you see yourself in long-term, your goal is to approach each segment of the rotation intending to perform such an outstanding job that every department is very interested in offering you a full-time position. Think of each rotation as a summer internship where you are trying to earn a full-time position. The truth is you are!

If you are interested in working full-time in one of the rotational areas, but the group is not interested in you, there will be no opportunity to work there. Mutual interest is a must. Bring your A game every day, have a great attitude, and try to get up to speed on the product, process, or basic content of the area as fast as possible. It is also important that you invest in building relationships within your group. Your goal is to make the other members feel that you are a natural part of the group and that you are not just passing through on a rotation. Demonstrate your value within your first month of the rotation.

Since most rotational assignments are three to six months each, you won't have much time to show the group how valuable you are. Taking four months of a six-month assignment to learn the product or how to execute tasks won't win you a position at the end of your rotation. If it is a three-month rotation through a group, you should endeavor to learn the basics about the group in the first two to three weeks. This way, by the end of the first month, one-third of the way through your rotation, you are demonstrating what you have learned and can "put a few points on the board," by completing all or part of an assignment or doing something else of value in the group.

How and Where You Enter an Organization Influences Your Compensation

Where and how you enter an organization also heavily influences your compensation, no matter if you are just starting out or if you are moving from one industry or job to another. Every job has a pay range that is considered "market rate" for that role. "Market rate" is the average pay range that most companies and organizations offer to people with comparable skill sets in comparable roles. In general, pay ranges are the same in similar geographic areas for comparable skills and years of experience. However, they can differ markedly across geographic regions, largely due to the differences in standards of living across the country and around the world.

A teacher with ten years of experience in New York City will earn $15–20K more than a teacher in Jacksonville, Florida, or Macon County, Georgia. That is because the cost of living in New York City is easily 40–50 percent higher. Someone entering a revenue-generating role at a company will likely enjoy a higher rate of compensation than someone entering in an administrative capacity, since the former is considered directly tied to the company's success.

If you join a company in an entry-level position, it is generally easier to be compensated near or at market rate. Generally, companies do not differentiate between employees at the entry level. For example, professionals entering a commercial bank in an entry-level training class will generally be paid the same salary and bonus. But as you rise to more senior ranks, the pay can vary from person to person, even if two professionals have the same number of years of experience or even hold the same title. The differential exists because someone believes that one person performs better than the other, or one professional may be better positioned politically than the other within the company. Do your homework and identify what the pay range is for the role you are interested in. Just as taking a job to get a foot in the door can prohibit you from eventually landing the job you really want, accepting a role with compensation below the market range will make it difficult for you to catch up over your tenure at the company. Even if your performance is outstanding over time, it will be difficult to recover salary if you start out at a deficit. Most companies have a precedent for the range of percentage increases in pay they will allow for employees. Even when you have a year of stellar performance above and beyond your contemporaries and the company rewards you at "the highest level" possible, that increase will probably still not bring your total compensation to market rate for that role because of where you started.

It's up to you to position yourself at the right compensation rate when you start your role. You must understand the value of the position and voice your desires when negotiating the numbers. Unfortunately, I have seen many professionals accept jobs at a lower compensation level during tough economic periods only to find themselves frustrated a few years later, after they realize they are earning far less than the market rate. At the time, they felt pressured to accept a job, thinking they should take whatever they could get.

While I understand that pressure, it is important to recognize that making this decision not only has current earning implications, it could also have significant implications for your future earning power at this company and with most prospective employers, who strongly consider your previous earnings when offering you a new position. Most organizations are willing to pay market rate for positions, particularly if the company's ability to compete depends on attracting and retaining the best and brightest within its ranks. Compensation is a part of the company's value proposition. However, during tough economic times, when unemployment rates are high and hiring has decreased significantly across industries, many companies will offer salaries near or below the low end of the compensation ranges for any given role.

Companies will take advantage of the demand/supply imbalance knowing that prospective employees are willing to make compensation concessions to land positions during tough times. That does not mean that you *have* to make a concession. If you are the best candidate for the position, *and* you can convince the interviewer that you will be a significant value add player for the organization, they *will* hire you at market rate.

When companies are preparing their expense budgets for the year and forecasting hiring as a part of that budget, they include numbers that are consistent with market rates. The bottom line is that they are prepared to hire you at market rate. But if they can do so at a cheaper rate, of course they will, that makes good business sense. Would you pay more than you have to if you were in a similar position? It is up to *you* to get to know your role and its market rate, and to have a strong argument for why you deserve it. It is a part of positioning yourself to successfully move forward in the organization.

Janet was interviewing for a position as the head of a nonprofit organization that helped customers rebuild their creditworthiness after home foreclosures, car repossessions, or other financial setbacks. Her previous experience included chief operating officer of a nonprofit that helped people find jobs after significant periods of unemployment, and before that she had worked as a commercial and consumer loan officer at a regional bank. The range of compensation for comparable nonprofit CEO positions in her geographic region was $140–200K. She earned $120K in her current position. In several conversations with interviewers at the potential new company, Janet was told that her credentials were outstanding, she was "perfect for the position," and that she was the best candidate they had seen during the process. When the chair of the board made Janet an offer of $130K, she stated it was "an almost 10 percent increase above your current salary and very generous given the tough economic environment."

Based on her research and conversations with executive recruiters specializing in nonprofit roles, Janet was shocked at the offer, knowing it was below market value for comparable CEO positions. Janet responded by saying, "Thank you very much for the offer to join the organization. I am excited by the opportunity and really enjoyed talking to the team. I believe I could be a great addition to the organization and could quickly execute on the board's vision for the future. This role is an important one and is comparable in its importance to other CEO and leadership roles in the state's nonprofit arena. Given the value of the role, I understand it to yield compensation in the range of $140–200K. It is very important to me that my compensation level is commensurate with what I am expected to contribute to the organization and I would be very excited to accept the position if the compensation were in this range."

The chair of the board cited again that the offer was above what Janet was currently making. But Janet pointed out that compensation for her current position reflected where she started in the organization, not the level of contribution and value she would bring to this new position. She reiterated her eagerness to take on the job and her confidence that she would make a significant difference to the nonprofit. In other words, she would create a terrific yield on the organization's investment in her. In the end, Janet received an increased offer that was within the market rate for the role.

Had Janet not done her research and known the market rate for the role, she might have accepted the lower offer, simply agreeing that it was an increase above her current compensation. She may have even complimented herself on getting an increase in a tight labor market. But even in such a tight market, companies are still looking for and hiring great people. You do not have to compromise on your compensation, but you do have to go into conversations about pay armed with the information necessary to have a powerful dialogue that will position you appropriately.

There are many online sources today that provide access to compensation ranges for almost any career. Visit sites such as salary.com or mercer.com, or speak to executive recruiters who know the market you are interested in. A good executive recruiter will be more than willing to speak to you because they want to find out who you are and whether you are someone they should have in their database and available to their prospective clients.

In fact, it is a good idea to maintain good relationships with executive recruiters throughout your career, as they can often be a good source of information regarding compensation levels for the various roles that might interest you. They can also keep you apprised of available job opportunities for people with your intellect and experience level. Your ability to position yourself for mobility within and outside of your company will depend on your network—your personal and professional relationships, including executive recruiters—and the kind of information you are privy to through those relationships.

I cannot stress enough how important it is to position yourself properly from a compensation perspective when you enter an organization, when you are just starting out in your career and, even more important, when you have had some experience and are changing jobs or fields. Prospective employers will always ask about your current compensation before presenting you with a formal offer for a new job. If you are too far behind what is considered market rate, it can handicap your compensation in the new job, or worse, it can create a perception about your capabilities or your ability to negotiate or speak up for yourself when it matters.

Linda began with her current employer twelve years ago in a very junior position. It was her first corporate job and she was excited to get an opportunity with one of her industry's leading companies. Linda has worked very hard over her tenure at the firm and has been given increasing responsibilities. But her pay increases have been comparatively modest, even though she now holds a very senior position in the purchasing department. Linda is being recruited for a head of purchasing position at another company in a completely different industry. Her prospective duties would be almost exactly the same as the ones for which she is currently responsible, but she would have to learn an entirely new industry. When her prospective new employer asked what her current salary was, he was astounded to learn it was 50 percent lower than what he expected. As a result, in the interview he started to question whether Linda was as good as she seemed to be. He could not reconcile how someone so talented could be paid at such a low level. Linda's failure to understand market rate and her value, and to negotiate for that rate as her experience and responsibilities grew, was threatening her ability to find another position (or, at a minimum, to get compensated fairly in the new role). Her current level of compensation cast a shadow of doubt on her judgment in the prospective employer's eyes.

How could Linda have better answered the interviewer's questions about her compensation? She could have said, "I do not think my current compensation level is as relevant to our conversation about this new role (and she did NOT have to disclose the number). When I started with my current employer, I was very junior and I accepted a role and a compensation level that was consistent with my experience. As I learned the job, I rose up through the ranks. Now as a more experienced professional, I would expect that in my next role my compensation will be commensurate with how the market currently values the skills and experience required for the job." This answer would communicate to the interviewer that perhaps she did not negotiate well as she began her career, but that she now understands her value and the value of the new position and has some compensation expectations about the job.

There are times when considering an offer that is below market rate may be appropriate. If you are switching careers and have no previous experience in a particular role and very little experience that is relevant to the new role, the employer is taking a risk on you. One could argue that they should be compensated for that risk in the form of paying you a slightly lower compensation than they would someone with experience and credentials for the job. In this instance, you are also investing in yourself by learning something new and positioning yourself for other roles in a new industry or in a new functional capacity.

This is similar to investing in yourself by going back to school for more education or training. It is important, however, that if you take on a role for less than market compensation, you have a very good idea of the opportunities to move within the organization or to higher compensation levels in the future. You don't want to find yourself in a position being paid at a discount for a long period of time or, as we've discussed, it will be difficult to play catch-up in later positions. In fact, when you are negotiating the salary, make sure to specifically acknowledge that you are accepting a below-market rate and come up with a specific time or performance milestone when you might revisit the compensation level.

Marie had been interested in arts management when she was in college, but felt that she should study something "practical" like finance, and then get a job in accounting so that she could earn a good, stable living. While she majored in accounting, she also took a number of classes in theater arts, management, and artist representation. After about eight years in her accounting job, she decided that she wanted a career change. She wanted to work in the business of the arts and to begin a career managing performance arts venues or individual artists.

Marie contacted some of her former college professors who had strong contacts in the performance world and asked for introductions so that she could start to network with these individuals and express her interest in working in the industry. She read industry magazines that related to performance venues and educated herself about the latest issues in the industry, so that she would have pertinent and intelligent questions to ask during her conversations with some of her new contacts.

About six months into her networking, one of the CEOs of a major performance venue needed an associate director and she was very interested in hiring Marie because they had really connected in their previous conversations. Marie came highly recommended by their mutual acquaintance, one of Marie's former professors. While the job was advertised with a compensation range that was inclusive and higher than what Marie was currently making in her accounting job, the CEO explained that the range was for someone who had previous experience in venue management.

Marie said that she recognized that she had a lot to learn about the industry and was willing to make the investment of the salary differential to learn in the short run. She negotiated that instead of a two-year review of salary and performance, she would have a twelve-month review of performance to potentially adjust her salary range to the lower end of what was normal for the role.

The Essential Skills and Exposure You Must Get

In almost every industry—technology, health care, retail, financial services, manufacturing, or media and entertainment—there are certain skills that people who ascend to the top of their companies or profession have in common. I call these *strategic skills*, the kinds of skills that you should seek to acquire very early on in your career. These skills include: *presentation skills*, the ability to speak effectively in front of groups of people; *management skills*, the ability to manage and lead a team to complete projects and objectives; *analytical skills* (or at the very least developing a comfort level with numbers); and *selling skills*, the ability to influence other people with your ideas. Even if you are one of the many people in recent years who have taken a job to get a foot in the door or a decent salary, you can position yourself to hone these skills and prepare for your dream job opportunity whenever it presents itself.

These skills are different from technical or functional skills (those that are specific to a functional area). For example, knowing bond math is a skill that you need to work on a fixed income trading floor or as an investment banker in public finance. But you might not ever use it if you are working in asset management or in mergers and acquisitions for an investment bank. Knowing how to build a story board is essential if you are working in advertising or maybe even consulting, but you will never use that skill if you are working in capital markets or operations in a logistics company.

From the time you begin your career up to the time you have about five years of experience, you should seek to get exposure to jobs or assignments that will offer you the chance to develop your strategic skills. They will be essential to your ability to move up in an organization and they will be valued by other buyers (employers) as you seek out opportunities. These skills are so important that even if you cannot get the job that you want, it is worth choosing a job that will let you acquire one or more of these strategic skills. When you are accepting a new position or assignment, it is important to look closely at the content of the job versus the job itself, and assess if it will give you one of these important skills, all highly valued in the market.

While the level of responsibility you'll have in a prospective role is important, it is critical that you evaluate your job opportunities by the kind of experience and expertise that you are likely to have when you finish in the role. As we've discussed, you have skills and experiences to offer a prospective buyer and your success depends upon your ability to effectively sell those skills. When you are considering a job opportunity, ask yourself if you are going to get exposure to or training in one of the aforementioned categories. If the answer is yes, then the job is a job worth considering, even if it is not the exact job that you want. You may also want to consider jobs that will give you opportunities for exposure to industries that you think that you might want to work in. That will ultimately help you decide if one suits you.

Consider Lizzie. As she prepared to graduate with her MBA she wanted to find a job in brand management at a major consumer products company. But given the economic environment, she could not seem to get an interview. None of the brand management companies were recruiting at her school that year.

Her job as a brand manager would be to create an appetite in the consumer for purchasing a given product and to be able to answer the question, "Why buy this brand?" Lizzie knew in order to get the position she wanted, she would need to know how to: market a product, position it competitively in the marketplace, and make it attractive to customers.

But with no success finding a position in her desired field, Lizzie began to look for other opportunities. There was a small nonprofit that had landed its first major donor and was poised to begin attracting more contributions. The organization had also just won an award for its outstanding GED program and its contribution to getting single mothers who didn't have high school diplomas into the workforce. What this organization needed was to raise its visibility in the philanthropic marketplace, and as a result gain greater exposure to potential donors. It needed a marketing plan to create and position its brand with major donors.

Lizzie took a marketing position with the nonprofit because she realized the role would give her the opportunity to get a key strategic skill: how to market and sell an idea to the marketplace. She worked side by side with the team's other members, including one who was a seasoned marketing professional, who had worked in brand management with a Fortune 500 for over twenty years before joining the small nonprofit.

Since the organization was small, the staff was small as well. Working closely with her colleague who had an extensive background in product marketing, Lizzie took on a good amount of responsibility and learned how to think about the organization competitively, how to compare and contrast it with other nonprofits, and how to articulate its differences in a compelling way (*product*). She learned about the levels of donor giving for nonprofits and how to study and differentiate the customer segments (donors) and how to learn what really mattered to them (*price*). She learned how to reach them, via the distribution channels that donors looked to for information about nonprofits (*place*). She also learned about developing a marketing message, priming media outlets for the organization's message, and about where and how often to deliver the organization's message (*promotion*).

In less than a year, she not only gained two of the key strategic skills, but also learned some of the fundamental skills she would have had she worked in a brand management program at a large consumer products company. Two years later, the economy had improved and Lizzie landed an interview at a global consumer products company. In her interview, she discussed how her integral role on a small team created a "brand" for a relatively unknown nonprofit. She discussed how she spent time researching media outlets, developing the organization's "story," and helping to sell it to potential donors.

Lizzie was also able to explain the importance of the concept of "hits" for the nonprofit's social media campaign that she helped create and promote. The campaign contributed to a 300 percent increase in donor contributions and a change in the demographic profile of its donors—all outcomes that were in large part due to Lizzie's work. She was offered and accepted her dream job, earning a spot in the brand management program for the global company.

Here is another example. Sam aspired to be a sales trader at a large investment bank. But he graduated in 2008, at a time when, due to the fiscal crisis, most investment banks were restructuring their organizations and resizing their trading platforms. In short, they were not hiring junior traders.

Sam understood that among the key skills a trading desk manager would find attractive were a passion for the markets and strong selling skills. Sam accepted a job in sales at a large pharmaceutical company that had a reputation for having one of the strongest sales training programs in the industry. He excelled, quickly becoming an expert in their biopharmaceutical products. Sam learned that the fundamentals of effective selling were understanding the customer's needs; knowing the key product facets that were most valued by the company; how to anticipate the points of debate around the product; and how to present his sales argument in a logical, cogent, and compelling way. Sam also worked at building relationships with people in the company's research area, and learned about early-stage drug products, the FDA approval process, and what large pharmaceutical companies looked for when developing or acquiring early-stage compounds.

After three years in this role, Sam was able to sell his sales experience, training, and knowledge of the pharmaceutical industry to a large broker-dealer who hired him as a specialized health care sales trader.

Like Lizzie and Sam, the key point to understand when you are early in your career is that focusing on the content of a job by gaining a valuable skill set is more important than the particular position. Even though Lizzie worked for a nonprofit organization instead of a consumer packaging or other company where she could engage directly in brand management and learn how to market products and sell ideas, she learned the essentials of marketing in that nonprofit role as she worked with an experienced professional who had brand management experience and who taught her the fundamentals of marketing: product, place, price, promotion.

No matter where you work, you can acquire and develop strategic skills. You can work in layout at a magazine, where you can learn management skills as the team, month after month, drives toward a deadline to get the magazine produced and distributed. You can take a job as a telemarketer and learn how to sell. You can take a job in the admissions office of a university or private school and acquire presentation skills as you go out to present the school to prospective students and their parents. If you can't find a chance to focus on desired strategic skills where you work, look for opportunities in your volunteer activities, at your church, or even with your friends. Practice presenting an argument to them and get their feedback to help you hone your presentation skills, lead the fund-raiser at your church to develop your marketing and sales skills, or run the next clothing drive at your school, which will give you management skills.

Many people looking for employment opportunities in a corporate environment never consider jobs at nonprofit organizations. However, it is possible to acquire some of the same skills you learn in the corporate arena by working at a not-for-profit.

For example, every nonprofit organization has a development function where professionals are required to research potential individual and institutional donors. In a development role, you would be required to create a strategic plan for approaching prospective donors. This would include executing a plan to meet with them, formally "make the ask" or solicit their financial support, ask them for their list of contacts, organize the data around donor follow-through, cultivate relationships, and ultimately increase the level of financial support for the organization.

In this function alone, you could acquire strategic planning, relationship building, analytical, presentation, and organizational skills, all of which you could use in almost any industry. It doesn't matter that you acquired these skills in a nonprofit environment, if you can articulate how applicable they are to a job in a for-profit entity (just as we saw with Lizzie). There are also finance, marketing, operations, and administrative roles in a nonprofit organization. The skills that are required to be successful in those roles are the exact same skills that you would need in a corporate environment.

Many companies have recruiting teams or employee resource groups. Volunteering to serve on your firm's recruiting team would give you practice in presenting—you would be making presentations to large groups of people about the advantages of coming into a specific industry and about joining your company in particular. You would also be selling candidates on the opportunity to work at your company after they have been given an offer. In fact, that was one of the ways I began to hone my own presentation and selling skills.

After graduation, I volunteered to be on my company's Harvard recruiting team (my alma mater). Soon, I found myself as the captain of the team. As captain, I had to marshal other volunteers, as well as enlist senior people when necessary to help sell candidates on coming to the firm (management skills). There was stiff competition for talent from other firms, and I took it personally if I lost a candidate to another company. I focused and became very good at selling my organization, rarely losing a candidate to a competitor (marketing and selling skills). Every year, out of eight to ten offers, I might lose one or two, but generally not to my direct competitor. My team consistently had one of the firm's best records for converting candidates to employees.

As I moved through my career in investment banking and had to sell companies and their stories to the market, I pulled from the persuasive selling skills I had developed while selling candidates to join the firm in my recruiting assignment. In learning to sell my firm to prospective recruits, I became skilled at developing compelling arguments about why they should work for the firm, and why they had to take the offer at that time versus revisiting the company at another time. When I was developing a sales story for a company that my firm was bringing to the public markets, the key components for the pitch to public investors were exactly the same: Why did they need to own the company's stock? And why did they need to own it now? Given my recruiting experience, it was relatively easy for me to develop these same pitches for prospective companies that we were introducing to the public markets.

So far, we've focused on the importance of acquiring strategic skills, which will be valued by an employer in almost any industry and will be useful to you and relevant to your success as you move throughout your career. I mentioned technical skills earlier and one of the key ways to get certain technical skills is through training programs at your job, or in your college or graduate school classes. Another way that you can acquire certain technical skills is to teach yourself. If you are interested in developing technical skills, such as with Microsoft Office or a specific programming language, but your functional job does not teach you or require you to use these skills, take an online course that will teach you Excel or PowerPoint or commit yourself to two hours every weekend to learn the skills from one of many guidebooks you can find. These are skills you can list on your résumé or discuss in a cover letter, even if they were not acquired in a particular job.

I have a friend who was a complete technology fossil. She barely knew how to turn on a computer! One day, she was asked to create a flyer and arrange for online payments for a fundraiser that her sorority was hosting. The organization could not afford to pay someone to do it. They wanted every dollar raised to go to their scholarship committee.

She went to the bookstore and purchased *Microsoft Office for Dummies* and committed herself to learning how to make a flyer. In fact, she became so proficient at creating promotional materials that she now runs a small side business performing similar tasks for other small nonprofits. And by the way, she was also promoted to a senior administrative position where she works full-time because of her demonstrated technological skills!

◄ *Carla's Pearls* ►

1. Taking a job to get a foot in the door may not lead you on a trajectory to a higher-profile or line role. Understand an organization's history with regard to promotions and job changes to avoid frustration when you try to make a move.

2. Rotational programs give you an opportunity to explore the company. Never view these assignments

as only a chance to get experience in that area. Do such an outstanding job at each one that each group is interested in hiring you.

3. How and where you join an organization influences your rate of compensation and can influence your future earning power. It's up to you to know the market rate for your position.

4. Don't just take any job. Even if it's not your dream, make sure it positions you well for what you really want to do.

5. The level of responsibility that you will have in a prospective role is important, but it is equally, if not more, important to evaluate your job opportunities by the kind of experience and expertise that you are likely to have when you finish in the role.

6. Make sure you acquire and develop strategic skills (basic selling, analytical, organizational, management, and presentation) and technical skills that are applicable and valued in many different jobs and industries very early on in your career.

7. Just because your functional job doesn't afford you the opportunity to learn or practice a skill you wish to learn, such as making presentations, doesn't mean you can't hone the skill elsewhere. Look for opportunities within the company to serve on teams or with employee groups to get experience. If you can't find opportunities where you work, consider using your volunteer activities, or other places where you give of your time, or even with your friends to learn and/or practice. Or commit time to try learning on your own by reading books or taking courses online or elsewhere.

STEPPING UP

CHAPTER 4

Managing Your Career

Performance Currency

*"Success is liking yourself, liking what you do,
and liking how you do it."*
—Maya Angelou

There is one person responsible for managing your career agenda, and that is YOU! Many people mistakenly think that the company they work for, specifically human resources, is responsible for planning out their careers and the moves and roles that they should take on. That is not the case. As we've discussed, early in your career is the time to focus on what kinds of skills and experiences you want to acquire. That way, two years in you are starting to build a solid tool chest of abilities and knowledge that you can use to sell your way into other opportunities. If you're further along in your career and haven't done this, don't worry—it's never too late to get started on building the skills that you want to acquire. If you are five, ten, or more years into working, develop a plan to get the skills and experiences you think you need and put yourself on a time line, seeking to get as many of your desired skills as possible within a two-year period.

The Career Agenda

As we briefly touched upon in Chapter 1, the current work environment offers a new approach to career planning. Unlike when I started working, I do not believe that today's young professionals should aspire to a twenty-five- to thirty-year career with one company (and as well, most people are retiring later than used to be the norm). Instead, people entering the workforce today should be planning for a career of six to eight modules of five years each at a different company. There is a case for you to decide to complete two or three of those modules at one company if the company is focused on reinventing itself and is committed to innovation, and therefore presents a compelling career proposition, but in most cases, you should seek to change companies at least three to five times over the course of your career in order to maximize your performance, power, pay, and platform of influence. If you have been working for a while, you should also be thinking about at least two to three changes during the rest of your career, assuming you are planning to work another ten to fifteen years.

Here's why.

To optimize your career platform (content, pay, influence, or seniority) you will most likely want to work for a leader in the industry in which you are interested. In today's economic environment, very few companies are able to maintain their leadership position unless they are doggedly, single-mindedly focused and committed to innovation and to reinventing themselves every few years. Many companies will not be able to make the commitment necessary to remain at the top of their respective industries due to financial or cultural constraints.

When you are thinking about your career agenda, consider the kinds of skills you would like to develop and how you can acquire them in as short a period as possible. In the first module of your career, as I said in the previous chapter, seek to gain strategic skills—basic marketing, selling, and presentation skills, an understanding of basic finance, and some exposure to strategic planning and human capital management, no matter what career vertical you are interested in. With these strategic skills, you will have the capacity to add value as you move to new areas where you may be required to focus on a particular expertise. I am a big fan of the building-block approach to your career, especially in an economic environment where it might be tough to get the dream job as you start out.

Let's say, for example, you would like a career as a fashion designer. Getting a meaningful job at a major label may be difficult to do right out of college, but let's think about the building blocks, the skills you can acquire that might make you an attractive candidate in the future.

When a label prepares to introduce a new product or line, they have to strategically consider how and when to introduce it to the market, and then advertise it. What medium will they use to launch? A major fashion show, television, social media, print? What is the strategy to get people to buy the new item?

These are some of the same considerations for introducing a consumer packaged product into the market. The first job that you take might be a job in brand management at a consumer products company, which would allow you to learn the fundamentals around managing a brand that would also be valuable when you have an opportunity to sell yourself to a major designer label. In addition, it might afford you the compensation that will give you the chance to take basic classes in patterning, draping, and merchandising and to acquire some of the other credentials that you will eventually need to be seriously considered a potential member of a fashion design team.

The key to creating a successful career agenda is to make sure that everything you are doing is leading you to your ultimate goal. You can use the worksheets that we discussed in Chapter 1—your Content Page, Jobs Page, and Skills, Experience, Education Page—to help you build this agenda. The job that you have today should either be fulfilling an agenda item that is about learning or mastering a skill, having a specific experience, achieving a certain compensation level or title, or positioning you for each of the above.

If you find yourself in a role that offers none of the above, then you will never maximize your professional success in the career vertical in which you are interested. It is time to leave that job, and quickly! Every year that you are in your career, you should be working toward what you want to achieve. If you are not, then it's a sure sign you are at a standstill and it is time to reconsider or rework your agenda. If you are just starting out in your career and you have aspirations to become a senior-level person in a specific industry, then the time line below is a loose guideline for managing your career. Again, it is most likely that by the time you have THE senior role, you will have worked for at least two or three companies in that industry. If you want to be on a track to have a senior-level position by the time you have seven to ten years of experience, you should be at a point in your career where you not only have a title three to four levels above an entry-level position but you are also managing people.

A straight-path, good corporate career agenda would look something like this:

Year 0–3:   Acquire basic strategic skills.
Year 4–7:   Promotion to a position of authority where you have at least a couple of people reporting to you.
Years 8–10: Run a group, division, or department, get management or supervisory experience.

Year 10+:   Have a senior-level title, opportunity to have a voice on the management team/committee of the company.

Year 15+:   Positioned for a C-suite opportunity.

With each level, you should have compensation expectations that are progressively, and markedly, larger. As we discussed in the previous chapter, understand what those levels are by researching industry sources and maintaining relationships with executive recruiters who can help you stay informed. If you are committed to the time line on your agenda, you might have to consider moving outside of the company to achieve your goals and you should start to explore moving at least a year before you are actually ready to go. (We will discuss change in Chapters 8 and 9.)

Perhaps you did not know exactly what you wanted to do when you finished college and you took a series of different jobs before settling on a career trajectory. In this case, your time line would look very different. However, the same message applies to you. If you did not acquire the basic skills in your early job experiences, you want to get as many of them as soon as possible. In addition you should seek to get decision-making or management authority within four to five years of embarking upon a new career path. In interviews, you want to emphasize your past experience (even if it is disparate) in other jobs and demonstrate how it has given you the ability to quickly contribute to your new role in a meaningful way.

Of course, if you aspire to be an entrepreneur, this agenda would look markedly different. But you should still have an outline of what you would like to accomplish and create a time line for developing your business, so you have a better probability of staying on target with your growth plans.

Performance Currency

Performance currency is the goodwill, reputation, and capital you create by doing your job well and creating stellar deliverables on discrete assignments. When you consistently complete assignments above expectations (for example, you complete it earlier than expected; add extra analysis or insight above what was asked for; or present information in a creative, clear, and constructive way beyond what your boss or the organization has seen before) you create performance currency.

Performance Currency = (Intellect + Experience + Strong Execution) x Multiple Occurrences

Webster's dictionary defines currency as "something that is in circulation as a medium of exchange." When you have a strong reputation and a track record of performance excellence, you can "exchange" it for a shot at a promotion, a coveted position on an internal task force, a raise, an introduction to more senior people in the company, a respected voice at the decision-making table (where people will listen to you and be influenced by your point of view in important discussions), a spot on the deal team for the next big transaction, an opportunity to present in front of the client, or a chance to recover if you make a really big mistake.

Performance currency is extremely valuable and there is no substitute for it. It is particularly important if you are in an environment where you do not have political power or an exceptionally strong standing. In the early days, in any environment, you don't generally have that kind of power. When you are new to an organization, it is very important for you to put points on the board early, to *earn* your performance currency. You must execute well the assignments that you have been given and both your boss and others should acknowledge that you have done so. You won't get promoted or be selected for assignments that could lead to promotions or give you greater visibility in the organization without earning performance currency.

It is important that you get the validation from your boss or someone with credibility and authority in your environment that you have performed well. That is part of what gives your performance currency some value. You may think that you did a great job, but if no one else thinks that it was a good job, or your effort or work was not valued by the organization, then your performance will not act as a means for promotion or higher pay, or a new opportunity.

Your boss can either acknowledge your performance formally in your evaluation appraisals, or they can do so informally, by telling you directly that you did a good job or by publicly acknowledging it in a group or department meeting. It is important that you hear from someone in the organization that what you have delivered to the organization is valued and meets or exceeds expectations.

Your performance currency can give you a voice as well as access to important internal relationships. Most people do not realize how important it is to start building this currency as soon as you join a company or department. It's human nature for people to start evaluating and measuring you as soon as you join any organization. If you are perceived to be having a hard time getting acclimated to the new environment or you appear standoffish, you are devaluing your currency before you even have a chance to build it. Similarly, if you make too many mistakes early on, people will decide that you are not as sharp as they might have anticipated or worse, that you are not a good fit for the organization.

We live in a fast-paced world, and unfortunately, perceptions and assumptions are made quickly. These misconceptions can damage your currency or make it hard for you to build it. Whenever you begin a new assignment or enter a new environment, take the first twenty-four to forty-eight hours to assess the easy points you can score right off the bat. Consider what small things you can do to send a message that you are the right one for this assignment and start building your performance currency.

You should also adopt an "under-promise and over-deliver" mentality, meaning you should always strive to deliver more than what was asked of you in an assignment. For example, if your boss asks for an assignment by 2:00 p.m., you should strive to have it completed by 11:00 a.m. If you are asked to create a summary of the research on a company, you may also want to hand in a summary on that company's biggest competitor and a quick comparative analysis of the two.

When you are completely new to an environment or industry, one easy way to start building performance currency is by asking the people you work with intelligent, perceptive questions about your assignment. If you are working with a new team, begin by asking your colleagues how they view your assignment and to define the most important milestones. When you ask perceptive, thought-provoking questions of the people you are going to be working with, you communicate that you have been thinking about the assignment and how to be successful at it. This will create a perception and expectation that you are going to do well.

Whenever I am the new girl on the block with a group of people who have already been working together, particularly if I am going to be leading them, I always first find out what *they* think about the assignment, what their expectations are, and what they expect of me as a leader.

Typically, my line of questioning goes like this: "What needs to happen in the next six to twelve months for us to say that this exercise or our performance together has been successful? How do we define success? More important, how is our customer (the boss, the clients, the market) thinking about success?"

If someone says, "We have to show that we have created efficiencies," then my next line of questioning is: "Well, how do we want to define efficiencies? Is it in shortening the process of production? Is it producing more quantities? Is it reducing cycle time? Is it being more transparent to the team? Is it being more transparent to the customer? How do *we* define efficiency?"

By engaging the group in the process of thinking about these questions and contributing to answering them, I am already starting to build some performance currency by defining success together with the group and engaging them in building a plan of action to attain it. It is important to note that this tactic will work for you whether you are the leader or just a member of the team. Never be afraid to ask thoughtful, informed questions. It's the easiest way to clarify expectations in any situation.

One of the most important things that you can do to build performance currency is to start defining what success looks like before you start to execute. Begin by getting agreement from those who will be involved with evaluating your success. Whether I am preparing to go into a client meeting, give a speech in front of three hundred people, or introduce myself to a group I will be leading or working with, I always ask myself, "What does success look like in this situation? What am I playing for and what is going to matter to the *people* involved in this situation?" If you can define it up front, then you can create a set of actions around that definition that you can then execute, allowing you to deliver a visible, identifiable success. The last thing you want to do is to begin working in a new environment without finding out what kind of work, behaviors, and assignments are valued in that organization, and how success is defined. If you don't have a sound understanding of what is valued there, you could find yourself working very hard without maximizing your success because you are working in a way that is inconsistent with the organization's definition of success.

I once had an assignment that involved pitching a product to a client for the first time. The firm had never done any business with this client, and no one had been successful in getting this client to even take a meeting with the firm. I failed to ask my boss the important question: What does success look like in this pitch? I jumped right in and began to work on a getting a meeting with the client, which I thought was a big deal, a huge win, since I knew no one had ever been able to get this client to meet with the firm to discuss this product. I aggressively used my network to get a warm introduction to the client and then finally convinced them to take a meeting with us and the product team.

We went in to pitch the idea, the meeting was successful, and we managed to get the prospective client to agree to a meeting with the product team. At the meeting, the head portfolio manager got into a philosophical debate with the client, where it became clear that the client did not like being challenged. In the end, they did not choose to engage in a transaction with us.

I later asked my boss about her views of the engagement with the client and she said that I had failed to deliver. I could not believe it! I had put in an enormous amount of work to get us that meeting—I had been resourceful, used my network, made an effective pitch to get them to agree to a meeting after I received an introduction, I prepped the team on what was important to the client, and did a great job on my part of the pitch, but in her eyes I failed because the client chose not to do the transaction.

I never had control over whether the client would ultimately decide to buy the product, but I could have an impact on whether they would even meet with us and I knew that there was real value to my firm in getting the exposure, since this was a client that the firm did not have a relationship with and it was a good candidate for other products that we sold.

Where I failed, however, was in getting my manager to define "the win" up front. Since I did not find out what was important to her in the end or try to redefine what should have been important, I left myself exposed to her definition of what success looked like and left my effort and my performance vulnerable to being undervalued or not valued at all.

What I should have done was gone to my manager and got her to agree that the "win" would be in obtaining the meeting, and getting the client to agree to a follow-up meeting would be yet another "win." I should have stressed the fact that no one at the firm had EVER gotten an audience with this client to discuss this product and that that in itself would be a huge win. After we obtained that win, we would work on other ways to successfully engage the client and each of those successes would be separately defined.

Do you see why? If I could convince my boss to redefine what would be valued, then I could have given myself a chance to earn performance currency. Since I could not control whether the client would ultimately buy the product AND no one else at the company had ever visited the client before, I should have separated the decision to buy the product from the decision to take the meeting. I could have then earned performance currency after each separate success.

Since I did not have this conversation with and agreement from my boss, she evaluated my success based on whether the client bought the product. Worse, I didn't receive any credit (earn any currency) for getting a first-time meeting with a high-profile client, developing a relationship that was tough to get access to, and teeing it up for the product experts to pitch the client in a subsequent meeting. Instead, the focus was on something I couldn't really control (in this instance, the sale). Instead, I could have been heralded for starting the relationship with a firm that has become an important client of the company, even though they did not buy the specific product in the first meeting!

Now let's think about Jan, a woman who is starting a new position as a salesperson in an asset management firm. In this job, Jan is responsible for exposing potential asset allocators to the products currently managed by the portfolio managers at her firm. Her ultimate goal is to convince clients to allocate some of their assets to a particular product.

Many considerations go into an asset allocator's decision, such as the portfolio manager's track record; the product's one-, three-, and five-year performance; the product's fees; the customer service offering; and the portfolio manager's actual presentation to the client. Many of the elements important to the client's buying decision are beyond Jan's control. Therefore, it would not be smart for Jan to position her success around the client's decision to buy or not. Rather, she should define her success as creating the opportunity to meet with the client to make a pitch. Jan should say to her boss, "Client X is looking to add a product to their allocation mix and I think ours offers a perfect opportunity. The client is going to run a competitive research process and getting an opportunity to pitch to them will be a challenge. But I would like to work on getting us a chance to tell our story, which will be a feat if we can pull it off. Would that be of value to the department?"

When Jan is able to get the meeting, she will be credited with the success of doing so and will earn performance currency. The reality of actually winning the business should be something that is defined in a broader way, but not directly attributable to Jan, since there are so many other factors beyond her control. Like Jan, you should always seek to find out what is valued by your boss on a given assignment. If you know what is valued (what deliverable, what action, what process), then you know what you need to accomplish in order to earn performance currency. If you do what I did, and just assume that you know what will be valued, then you can expend a lot of effort, perform well in your execution, but not earn the currency that you need to trade to better assignments, different roles, or higher pay and promotions.

Influencing Your Environment

It is clear that you can create performance currency by delivering on a project or assignment. The next important development in stepping up in your career is moving from having a reputation of being a high performer to having a reputation as someone who has influence in the environment. Having influence in an organization can rapidly expand your performance currency.

As I stated earlier in this chapter, once you acquire performance currency, you can use it to assert your voice at work to influence the environment, which can impact ways that you can contribute to the organization's efficiency, bottom line, acquisition of new clients, or ways that you can put your own stamp on your department or company. After you have acquired performance currency, you should be actively looking for ways to start to influence changes in your environment.

In order to do this, you must know and understand the dynamics and culture of the organization; understand who the key players are; know what to communicate, and when, where, and

how to communicate it; and last, understand how to categorize
your idea for the best implementation. Generally however, unless you are the boss you cannot create change without collaborating with other people and building momentum around the
changes that you would like to make. As with anything, there
are tools and strategies that will allow you to tactically and effectively communicate your innovative ideas. They involve: 1)
identifying the type of idea; 2) recognizing "the players" in the
environment; and 3) developing a strategy of communication
with each of the players.

The Idea Type: Evolutionary vs. Revolutionary

All ideas can be categorized in two ways: evolutionary or revolutionary. An evolutionary idea is one that is really not new at
its core, but instead builds upon, enhances, or improves an idea
or concept that already exists. An evolutionary idea does not
require a change in thinking or the way of doing things, adoption of a new behavior or actions, nor does it dictate or force
change. If you are introducing an evolutionary idea into your
work environment, you should make sure to include the existing idea as a part of your presentation of the new idea, in order to remind people that they already embrace the core idea
and that your suggestion is simply the next stage of development
for the product or process.

The first thing to do when trying to sell your evolutionary
idea into the environment is to identify the author of the original idea if the idea was created at your company. You want to
position your conversation with that person so that it includes
accolades about the existing process and mention how it motivated you to see how you might be a part of enhancing it further. Notice, I did not say that you should say or imply that

anything is wrong with the current implementation of the idea. Instead, you want to suggest that you were motivated to see how you could "be helpful in making it even more valuable to the organization."

You then offer your idea to the original author and ask for his or her feedback. Toward the end of the conversation, you want to directly ask for that person's support of your enhanced concept and tell them about your plan to offer it up for consideration. Ideally, you would like them to cosponsor the enhancement in its introduction to the organization.

In effect, you are leveraging the currency of the person who originated the idea to influence the work environment. Even though you may have developed the idea for the improvement on your own, don't be preoccupied with sharing credit with someone else. Remember, the goal is to influence your environment for the better and create greater performance currency for yourself. It will not hurt you AT ALL to share credit with someone else. One hundred percent of 0 is 0!!! A percentage of something that is valuable is always better than nothing and you will receive even greater endorsement from the organization because you have shared the credit with someone who already has capital.

On the other hand, a revolutionary idea is an idea that involves change and is completely new to the organization. A revolutionary idea will require that people do things differently, perhaps analyze things differently, or even look at different kinds of data. It's much harder to get others to absorb this kind of idea because, in general, people don't like change.

When you are trying to get people to change, you have to give them some incentive. That incentive can be positive or negative, but it should be consistent with the organization's culture. For example, if your culture is one where people are motivated by positive stimuli, or "the carrot," then you should consider offering something positive. If on the other hand, your culture is one where people are motivated by negative stimuli, or "the stick," then you can use fear or the threat of losing something to get people to adopt the idea.

Here is an example: Fred is the sales manager at a wireless communications company where the salespeople are paid a commission on every phone they sell. Fred would like to get them to sell a certain brand of phones, so he has offered 10 percent extra commission for every one of these phones that are sold. This is a revolutionary idea, because the salespeople were being asked to sell one particular phone over another, when they had never been asked to do this before.

Fred was trying to create a change in behavior. He used a positive stimulus, a premium commission, to create the change. In this case, it is easy to see that a positive stimulus would be the best tool to create change, because there was clear evidence that the salespeople would respond to commission incentives. As a result, the salespeople sold one and a half times as many of that brand as they did the other phones that were available in the store.

Lucy is the chair of a loan review committee at her firm. The process for a loan review committee meeting has historically been to set aside a time for the deal team to give an oral presentation about the loan transaction. These meetings are generally long because each committee member has a number of questions about the company, the deal structure, the risks, the intended distribution process, and any potential liability for the firm. Lucy developed a memo format that included all of the key deal issues to make it easier for the committee members to review the information prior to the meeting, allowing them to focus the meeting on the most important issues and in a more efficient manner.

When Lucy tried to implement the new process and get the

deal teams to do the work for the memo, she met with a lot of resistance. The teams did not want to take the time to do the extra premeeting work. Lucy realized that the only way that she was going to get her idea implemented was to tell the teams that they could not meet with the committee unless they prepared and distributed the deal memo beforehand. As soon as she denied the request of several teams to meet with the committee until a memo had been submitted, the deal teams started to follow the new process.

In this case, Lucy introduced a revolutionary idea—she wanted the deal team to implement a new process that would involve preparing memos and doing work that they had not done before. In order to get them to change, she used a negative stimulus—denying them access to the committee members and prospective approval in order to motivate a change in the behavior.

When you want to influence your environment and it involves a radical change, you have to not only sell the idea, but you must have a cogent argument about why the change is necessary. Before you start to sell the idea, think carefully about who wins and who loses if things are going to be different. If everyone wins with the new change, then you need to make sure that the implementation of the change is an easy one for people to adopt. If someone is going to win but others will lose, then you have to make sure to gather other people to help you sell the idea to those who will be unhappy with the change. Generally this is hard to do effectively on your own. If the change will involve some inconvenience and discomfort for everyone in the organization, then you should have a very strong argument for the positive elements of the change for the company and enlist the help of other, more powerful players in your organization.

The Players: The Sponsor, the Supporter, the "Say No to Everything" Person, the Saboteur

In every organization, there are four types of people you will have to work with who can affect your ability to step up and influence your environment, and who will ultimately have an impact on your success: the sponsor, the supporter, the saboteur, and the "say no to everything" person.

The sponsor, which I covered in detail in *Expect to Win*, is the person who is "carrying your paper into the room." This is the person at your job who will spend their valuable political and social capital on you behind closed doors. They should be passionate about your strengths and be a huge supporter for your ability to move up in the organization. The profile of a good sponsor is someone who is internal to your environment, has exposure to your work, has a seat at the decision-making table, and has the "juice" to help you ascend in the organization.

Whether you have an evolutionary or revolutionary idea, you should always speak to your sponsor about it first. It is important that you try the idea out with them so that you can get a pretty good read on how the rest of the organization might react or what the challenges might be. Your sponsor can help you craft a message to the rest of the players in the organization, allowing you to maximize your opportunity to have the idea embraced by others. They can also advise you on the best timing for the message, which is important, especially with respect to when you communicate it to the key players. You wouldn't want to deliver a new idea that involves an increase in health care costs right after the company has announced across-the-board reductions in annual raises.

The supporter can be someone who is senior or junior to you, or they can be a peer. They are generally in agreement with any suggestions that you make in meetings, are willing to back you in the organization with respect to your new ideas, and always have something positive to say about you, even when you are not present in the conversation. You should always endeavor to speak to your supporters after you have your sponsor on board. Ideally you would like them to start spreading your idea, positioning it with positive messages in their networks before you announce it a large meeting or in a more public forum than one-on-one conversations.

The "say no to everything" person is someone who has a negative attitude toward almost any new suggestion. It doesn't matter who puts forth a new idea, this person always has a reason for why it won't work. This person can be very detrimental to your ability to influence your environment. Depending on the amount of currency that they have and whether other people are already skeptical about your idea, the "say no to everything" person could potentially sway them to reject it. You should only speak to the "say no to everything" person after you feel comfortable that your idea has been fully embraced by your sponsor and a large number of your supporters. But speaking to them is important, because their objections might reveal potential blind spots in your idea and implementation plan. Talking to them in advance of your official presentation to the organization will allow you time to prepare a counterpoint to their issues and avoid being blindsided in a critical meeting.

The saboteur is someone who does not like you and looks for opportunities to oppose any idea or to criticize any action that you attempt to execute at work. This person may feel that they have a legitimate reason to not like you or they may be afraid of you, believing that you have the power to inhibit their ability to get recognized or move ahead. Sometimes this person is easily identified because they make overt actions to sabotage your work or your ideas. Other times, they may be passive and covert in their efforts to oppose you.

Of the four personality types, the saboteur is not present in most environments. It's rare to find someone who is actively working against you. However, these people do exist and from time to time you will come across them. And this is why I think it's important to identify them as a player in the environment, so when you do come up against them, you will recognize them and understand how to maneuver around them.

The Strategy of Communication: How, Where, What, and When to Communicate?

After you have categorized your idea as evolutionary or revolutionary, and you have a pretty good idea who the players are in your environment, then you must develop a strategy for how you will communicate your ideas to each of the players and to the organization. Chronologically, you want to speak to each of the players for the reasons that we discussed, before you introduce your idea to the broader organization or in a meeting. Let me be clear: I am not suggesting that you tell every person in your environment that fits into one of the categories but rather a handful of people, so that you can get a solid idea of how your idea will be received and whether it will be embraced.

You should speak to no more than two of your sponsors, two to three of your supporters, one saboteur (if any), and one to two "say no to everything" players. This should give you a strong idea of the kind of support that you are likely to receive as well as an idea of any criticisms or derailing comments that could potentially arise.

How Do You Communicate?

If it is a revolutionary idea, one of the most effective ways to communicate is in the form of a question:

- Why do we implement the process this way?
- When was this process introduced?
- Has anyone ever tried to refine the process?
- Is it possible to make this eleven-step process more efficient by making it an eight-step process?
- Have we thought about using technology to streamline this process?

Where Do You Communicate?

- Inside the meeting room
- In open forum
- Outside the meeting room
- Off premises

What Do You Communicate?

When you are introducing a new idea, it is important that you can clearly answer the following questions:

- What is the idea?
- How does it work?
- Why does it work?
- Why is it necessary?
- What resources are needed to make it work?
- What is the time line for implementation?
- Why is it worth a try?
- What are the consequences if doesn't work?

- How/when will you shut it down if does not work?
- How will you measure success?

When Do You Communicate?

- At Town Halls in the form of a question
- Before the formal meeting where you will present the idea
- During a time of change at the company
- After the company has made a big positive announcement

Before you introduce change into the environment you want to have a very clear understanding of why things have been done the way they have. They might be the way that they are for a specific reason, and that could be why everyone has embraced the current process. Knowing the history will help you understand how to sell the change. On the other hand, perhaps no one has ever questioned the current process and a real opportunity exists to change it. No one will respect your idea or you as a change agent unless you demonstrate that you understand the history of why something is the way it is. Understanding and articulating the background will help you leverage your argument about why it might be time for your innovative idea. Remember, if you want someone to change something you have to make it worth their while, sell the idea, and understand the positive or negative incentives that will make them change.

If your idea is an evolutionary idea, then you can introduce the idea by making a suggestion. You can say something like, "I was speaking to Ed, who created the process that we use today, and we were discussing that perhaps we could continue to evolve the process by doing the following three things." Remember, the key to selling an evolutionary idea is to refer back to the existing one, with which people are already comfortable. Use that existing positive place as your launch pad. Ideally, if you can use the original architect as part of your sale then that will be most helpful. If not, you must make the idea sound like it is an easy transition from where the organization is to where you want it to be.

Assuming that everything is going well in your work environment, you should introduce your idea as soon as you have refined it, can articulate the pros and cons, have developed an implementation plan and identified the resources needed to implement it, and have some idea of how its success can be measured.

You never want to introduce an idea when you haven't thought through these issues. When you approach your sponsor or supporters, they will likely ask you about them. While you always want to leave room for others to contribute, change, or further develop your idea, you never want to appear to have a half-baked concept where you haven't considered the important elements associated with implementation or the implications of your idea. Doing so could make it difficult for you to garner the support you need to influence and introduce the idea into the environment.

When an organization is in some kind of a crisis— experiencing bad publicity, for example, resulting from some kind of public scandal—that is often an opportune time to introduce a revolutionary idea into the environment. When things are chaotic, leadership is looking for innovative ideas and solutions that could help solve a crisis or create an opportunity to turn things around. If an organization is in a predicament, the same old solutions won't help solve the problem. As such, new ideas and innovative solutions are often embraced.

Alternatively, when your organization is performing at record levels, when revenues and profitability are at an all-time high, and it's enjoying industry-leading recognition or a growing customer base, there is usually a pool of resources available to invest in and implement new ideas. This, too, can be a great time to introduce both revolutionary and evolutionary ideas.

If the opposite is true, and the economic environment is poor, the company will be rationing resources, at which time it is okay to introduce an evolutionary idea into your environment, particularly if it positively impacts expenses and introduces cost savings. However, a challenging economic situation is not the best time to introduce a revolutionary idea because people are generally fearful and are trying to execute their jobs with fewer resources.

When you are selling a new idea, either evolutionary or revolutionary, you should be able to answer all of the questions above, particularly if you are talking to a senior decision maker about the concept. The whole point of stepping up and influencing your environment is to help position you to ascend in your workplace. Part of demonstrating your leadership and your talent is showing that you can not only create ideas but that you are also smart enough to think through how these ideas might be implemented, and how and why they are valuable to the company. Part of enhancing your currency is demonstrating that you are thinking of ways to enhance not only your value but the value of the company or the organization as well.

Recovering from a Mistake

Understand that there will be times you step up, introduce a new idea, and frankly, fail. Perhaps there were some unforeseen variables that derailed your plan. Whatever the case, introducing the idea when you did turned out to be a mistake.

Everyone makes mistakes. And you should not let doing so completely unsettle your career. It is not the act of falling that is the problem, but rather not getting up after you do. Performance currency is valuable in your recovery. If you make a mistake and you have a reputation for producing high-quality work or making high-quality contributions in your organization, then people will forgive or overlook a couple of missteps.

The trick in recovering from a mistake is to: 1) own up to making it; 2) articulate what you learned from it, either to your boss or in a public way; 3) correct the error; and 4) endeavor not to make the same mistake again.

 *Carla's Pearls*

1. The three keys to successfully managing your career are: your career agenda, performance currency, and using that currency wisely. Performance currency is that goodwill, good reputation, and good capital you create by executing your job well and creating stellar deliverables on discrete assignments.

2. It is important to start building performance currency as soon as you join a company or department. Putting points on the board immediately will go a long way to helping you establish yourself in a new environment.

3. You must define success in a way that you can deliver and that will allow you to create performance currency by delivering a visible, identifiable achievement.

4. Influencing your environment creates greater performance currency. There are three keys to successfully influencing your environment: categorizing your idea as evolutionary or revolutionary; identifying and

properly communicating to the players; and knowing how, where, what, and when to communicate
your idea.

5. There are four types of players in any environment:
the sponsor, the supporter, the "say no to everything"
person, and the saboteur. You need to know the best
way to deal with each type.

6. Making mistakes is common in any workplace. What
is important is how you recover.

CHAPTER 5

Starting to Build Relationships

Relationship Currency

"Build the right relationships with the right people and nurture them over time and you'll always have a leg up on the competition."

—Paul May

Relationship currency is very different from performance currency. In this case, the relationships that you have are the medium of exchange you use to further your professional agenda; to acquire more responsibility, more senior roles, and better assignments; and even to have your voice heard.

Relationship currency is measured by the strength of the relationships you have developed and what leverage you have because of those associations. Building relationships in an organization is as important, if not more important, than your performance on the job.

I have often heard people say, "I don't need to go out of my way to build relationships, I will just let my work speak for me." If I had ten dollars for every time I heard someone say this phrase, I would be a very rich woman! There are so many professionals who convince themselves that if they produce high-quality work they will be rewarded, and that building relationships is not necessary because the quality of their work will speak for them. They think their good work alone will mean they will be well compensated and promoted. Well, the truth is, in the early days of your career, as we discussed in the last chapter, doing good work will get you noticed and maybe even rewarded, but it won't be the strongest currency for helping you reach the more senior levels or for getting you access and exposure to other opportunities.

As you get more and more senior in an organization or you aspire to acquire a senior-level position, more of the decisions about promotions are increasingly made based on judgment, and judgment is influenced by relationships. Everyone else who you are competing against is presumably good at their job. What will make the difference between choosing you over another candidate is the power of the relationships that you have.

As you ascend to more senior levels in an organization, the people evaluating your candidacy are looking at attributes that relate to your management skills, your ability to influence, and your ability to organize, motivate, and execute. Your technical skills, while important, are not as valued, and are frankly assumed as a part of your portfolio of skills. The way that people make assessments of your capabilities in these areas is by observing you, working with you, spending time with you—in other words having a RELATIONSHIP with you.

With Whom Should You Have Relationships?

When you first join a company or organization, you should immediately start to build relationships and networks. As I discuss in *Expect to Win*, your networks should be horizontally and vertically broad and should span all levels within the organization. In other words, they should include people who are senior to you; your peers and people who are junior to you; people within your department and division; and people from other parts of the organization.

The relationships within these networks are important because they can provide three things for you: 1) access to people you need to know; 2) information you need in order to successfully execute an assignment or move ahead; and 3) the assurance that you need when you are not sure how to read a particular situation.

In most organizations, departments are interdependent. There- fore, seeking to have relationships with every department that touches yours, or as I like to say, every seat that touches your seat, is important. For example, in a publishing house, the editor is re- sponsible for making sure that a book has the right content and flows well, but the marketing department decides how the book should be positioned competitively. Based on their knowledge of previously published books and those that will come to the market around the same time, they will give input on the cover and will pitch ideas to the sales team. And then the sales team will help de- cide when to release the book, in what season, what month, and around what promotions. And still yet another group, the publicity department, works closely with the marketing department to de- cide how to promote the author and book—through what chan- nels, and how to prepare the author for appearances.

As the editor, you are ultimately responsible for that book's success. If you don't have strong relationships with everyone in this operational loop, the success of your book and your ul- timate job success will be compromised. As you invest in the skills that you need to be a great editor, you must also invest in the relationships that support you in that success. There is no position within any company that is a stand-alone position; there is always another role that supports its success.

Think of a hospital. While the surgeon is important to the execution of the surgery, he or she cannot be successful if the an- esthesiologist does not administer the right amount of medica- tion to the patient, or if the nurse fails to properly prepare the

IV or prep the patient for the procedure. Each person in the organization plays a role and is in some way responsible for a successful outcome for the patient. Each of these relationships is important to the chain.

In many cases, top surgeons will choose who will assist him or her in a surgery. If you have a great relationship with the surgeon and your skills are deemed to be as good as or better than the other nurses or anesthesiologists, then the surgeon is likely to request you to work on his or her team. Your relationship currency will buy you the opportunity.

How Do You Acquire Relationship Currency?

Relationship currency is created by spending time with people in your organization, getting to know them, sharing ideas with them, or working with them on internal task forces and other company projects. If you consistently have positive interactions with someone, getting to know them beyond their professional title or function—where conversations expand beyond perfunctory professional chatter—will help you start to build a solid relationship. The process for building professional relationships is similar to the way you build them in your personal life. The best ones generally include "frequency of touch," or frequent and regular interactions and/or shared experiences.

I often hear people say, "My relationships are not very strong at work. I don't have anything in common with the people who I work with." If you find yourself making this statement, I would argue that the issue is not that you don't have anything in common with your coworkers, but rather that you have not invested any time toward building relationships with them. You already have SOMETHING in common with the people you work with simply because you work for the same company. Remember, when you were hired, one of the factors the interviewer considered as part of the decision to hire you was Your Fit. You got the job because the interviewer thought that you had characteristics that were in common with other people who were already part of the team. It is rare that relationships, personal or professional, develop or strengthen without a concerted effort. You have to put in effort to keep work relationships relevant and current, just as you have to do in your personal life.

This is especially true when you are new to a work environment. One of your first tasks should be to immediately start to build connections within and outside your department. Most people start a new job and focus only on specific job-related accomplishments. They very rightly want to put points on the board and create performance currency as soon as possible. While we've discussed the importance of doing so, ignoring opportunities to build relationship currency as soon as you join an organization is a mistake.

If you are on the shy side, or it is not natural for you to casually invite people to lunch or coffee, then you'll need to create some discipline around doing so. Create tasks on your calendar that will prompt you to reach out to someone with an invitation once a week. When I first began my career, it was not easy for me to reach out to my colleagues, especially those who were senior to me. But I realized that if I did not have relationships with certain people, I might not be considered for particular assignments and opportunities in the future. Further, I might not have access to the information that was often circulated informally among the other associates during more casual interactions. My solution to this problem was to literally put dates on my calendar where I planned to focus on getting to know people. I would write: March 12, Ask Person A out for coffee. Then follow up with coffee again with Person A on April 22. And ask them to lunch on May 16.

I took deliberate steps to remind myself to make these dates, because I knew that if I didn't, three or four months would go by and I would still not have started developing a relationship that I thought would be important to me. Especially if you are not working directly with or don't have a natural way to enjoy frequent interactions with someone you want to get to know, you have to create these opportunities.

When I was a young associate, I thought the more senior people in the firm should reach out to me. After all, I was the "new girl on the block." I thought they would want to build a relationship with me and offer me advice about how to be successful in the business and within the firm. I was very naive!

Once I realized it was my responsibility to make connections with these individuals, I found the majority of them to be accommodating. They were glad to meet with me and share some of their perspectives about the firm. As very busy senior professionals, they assumed that if I wanted to take advantage of their experience and perspective, *I* would make the effort to reach out to them. As I've taken on more senior roles myself, I've started to understand that perspective even more. While my own calendar has become increasingly busy over the years, I remember my initial perspective as a young associate and try to be proactive about meeting with new people in my organization and also put the word out that I am accessible and always willing to help others with their careers.

Still, even when you make a concerted effort, making connections can be tough. When I was a vice president and I first started to price transactions on the syndicate desk in Equity Capital Markets there was a trader with whom I wanted to build a relationship. He had a reputation for being a difficult person to work with, but was considered one of the best traders on the desk. He could, in my opinion, make the difference in how a deal opened in the market the day after pricing. I really wanted to forge a relationship with him so that I could request, when possible, that he be the guy opening my deals on the exchange the morning after pricing a transaction.

The first few times I approached his desk to talk to him, he was dismissive. I would stand by his chair attempting to get his attention to ask a question or to talk about the deal I was working on and he would act as if I was not there. Now, I am an African American woman of a good height. There was no way that he could miss me, particularly on a trading floor with a lot of other people that look nothing like me. Not to mention I was usually only standing twelve inches from his chair!

Yet he would speak to other people, talk to his desk mate, and sometimes even get up and walk away as if I were invisible! So what did I do? I started paying attention to the times he usually would go for coffee. Close to his usual mid-morning time I would stop by and say to him and some of his desk mates, "I am headed to Starbucks for a coffee. Can I get you one?"

Invariably the other guys would say yes, and then he would agree. When I returned, I used the interaction as an opportunity to compliment him on one of the deals he had opened that week; bring up a recent sports event; or ask a question relating to his business. I did this over and over again, until it felt like no big deal for the two of us to have a conversation. If I was on the trading floor to see someone else, I would make a special trip to say hello to him and the others. I used frequency of touch to help expand and build our relationship. I created a reason (the coffee) to have frequent interactions with him, discussed various topics with him, but most of all, invested time and effort into the relationship. Over time, he would even buy me coffee!

I used what I knew: traders don't often leave their desks, making them somewhat of a captive audience; they tend to be busiest at the market's opening and its close, so I stopped by when I knew they'd likely be free; and that, in general, topics like sports or their last deal were good ways to start a discussion.

I capitalized on those to create frequent interactions, and eventually a relationship began to develop.

If you want to get to know someone, for whatever reason, you can't sit back and wait for them to reach out to you. The truth is, they may never do so. As we discussed in the previous chapter, YOU are responsible for your career. You are the one that needs a portfolio of relationships to be successful. As a result, it is up to you to be proactive about building the relationships you need.

Don't be put off if you make an overture to begin a conversation or forge a relationship and the other person's reaction is not what you hope. Sometimes, people are just as nervous as you are about talking with someone new. They might not know how to react and may seem reluctant to talk to you at first. Or some people just do not want to take the time.

My advice? Go forward with your conversation anyway. Once you finish the conversation, you can move on to the next person, but don't shy away because someone is rude. Be who you are no matter what others are doing. It is your goal to build a relationship, so you try your best. Every time you try, it will make you more comfortable in your next conversation with someone else. If the person does not respond after repeated attempts, you could ask them directly if there is a reason the two of you are having a hard time connecting, or you can simply move on to attempting to pursue relationships with others who may be tangential to that person. It's up to you.

There will be some cases where someone of influence whom you may be interested in getting to know may be difficult to connect with because either the culture doesn't accommodate an open-door policy, making it hard for you to just go to their office for an informal meeting; or because there is no real business reason for you to interact. However, let's assume you are connected to other people who often interact with the person you want to meet. When talking with those people, mention that you are interested in meeting the more senior person. Ask questions about what they are like to work with and ask for advice on how to approach them. The people you know will more than likely broker an introduction for you or give you advice on how to approach the person yourself.

It's important to keep in mind that if you are using someone else's relationship currency to build your own, you should handle it carefully. Make sure to put your best foot forward when you finally get your opportunity to meet the person you seek to build a relationship with. Have topics ready that cover a five- to seven-minute conversation. Your goal should be to get enough information in that first conversation that will help you to have a second one. You want to start to build a way to have frequency of touch and to make sure each subsequent interaction is a positive one.

Performance currency, which we covered in Chapter 4, is another route to solidifying relationships. You may find that you are repeatedly assigned to work with certain people or on certain types of projects. Not only will these repeated interactions offer you the opportunity to get to know others and build strong relationships, but when you consistently work with someone and produce stellar work that reflects well on them, you will find that they will increasingly begin to trust you. They'll be more willing to support your point of view in meetings; they may suggest you for promotions or new assignments; and they may even be willing to support you behind closed doors, acting on your behalf when you are not in the room. Why? Because they like and trust you, appreciate the work that you have done for them, and feel a strong affinity toward you and your professional welfare.

The Trust Factor

One of the things that causes professionals to have trouble developing and building meaningful relationships is lack of trust. If a professional feels that they have been slighted at work, treated un-fairly, or his or her confidence has been betrayed, then they start not to trust specific individuals; and before long, they start not to trust the environment that they work in. If someone feels that they can't trust the environment that they work in, they typically will start to pull back from investing in relationships. They won't share much about who they are and won't engage authentically in interactions with peers, people more senior to them, and sponsors. This is all counterproductive to acquiring relationship currency.

If this happens to you, please remember that you can't let one or two interactions cause you to mistrust your entire or-ganization or department. If you do not trust the environment, then you will be guarded and not fully engaged and eventually that will compromise your overall success. People who might be interested in building a relationship with you, or even better, sponsoring you, will be hesitant to do so because they can sense your hesitancy to interact with others.

Trevor had a tough boss who he felt had never really sup-ported him to move ahead in the organization. His boss was often critical of his work, sometimes embarrassed him in meet-ings, but yet kept requesting Trevor to work on his projects. Trevor had been with the organization for two years. He felt that he had done a stellar job and had invested in his projects over and above what was required of him. As a result, he felt that it was time for him to be promoted to the next level. How-ever, when he approached his boss about moving to the next level, he was told, "We'll see."

At the end of the year, when promotions were announced, Trevor's name was not on the list and he was angry. He also did not trust that his boss would support him the next year. Trevor took an "I will just do my job and no more" attitude and began to withdraw from engaging in the organization. He spent very little time with coworkers, and did not meet with colleagues outside his department nor with people more senior to his boss.

He came in every day, did what was assigned to him, and then left every day at 5:00 p.m.

Within the next twelve months, Trevor was feeling stuck and trapped in his role. He had no relationships to help him create a pathway to move outside of his current role because no one really knew him. After being disappointed by his boss, Trevor did not trust the environment enough to engage with anyone else to build the kind of relationships that were essential to his ability to move within the organization.

You may think you can fool people, pretending to engage colleagues while you really keep them at arm's length. And while you may be able to do this for a short period of time, you won't be able to continue to play the role over the long haul. If you have had an incident that impacts your trust in the organization, I would challenge you to reassess the incident and discern if it is a systemic issue in the entire organization, or rather one or two people with whom you have a conflict. If the latter is true, work to move beyond the incident and seek to build authentic relationships with others. If you really feel that you cannot trust the entire organization and believe its values and vision are no longer aligned with yours, it might be time for you to make a change. It is important that you feel comfortable enough in your environment to invest in and build relationships that will be helpful to you in moving ahead in your career.

Three Things Relationship Currency Can Do for You

Once you have built true relationship currency, its power will motivate people to act on your behalf. Relationship currency can give you the ability to: 1) request something or some action of someone else; 2) connect to other relationships; and, as we discussed with regard to performance currency, 3) recover from a mistake.

If you have established a strong relationship with someone, you can ask them to do something on your behalf. The some-thing could be as simple as asking them to cover your shift, give you information, or show you how to do a task that will help you complete an assignment. Or it could be something more significant, such as asking someone to support your candidacy for a promotion or for a new assignment.

Every professional environment is made up of tangible work product and subjective judgments. Judgments are made and in-fluenced by people, and oftentimes your relationships can influ-ence someone's judgment on your behalf.

When I first started my career, we did not prepare our own client presentations. There was a group of people who made up a word processing department that was tasked with preparing presentations. Whenever anyone submitted a presentation, it would go into the queue to be worked on in order of when it was received.

Every time I went to that department, I would take the time to talk to the professionals who worked there. We'd often spend ten to fifteen minutes chatting about the firm, a recent movie, their families, our outside interests, and so forth. Over time, I estab-lished pretty good relationships with almost everyone in the de-partment on both the day and night shifts. There were several occasions when I was working on a transaction and my manager would decide to make some last-minute changes to the client pre-sentation that was due in, let's say, three hours. I would hurry down to the word processing department, only to find a long queue in place and an estimated five-hour turnaround time at best.

While I did not do it often, if the situation was really dire I would ask my word processing colleagues if they would make an exception for me and move our presentation ahead in the queue. They helped me meet my manager's deadline every single time. Why? Because we had a relationship. Had I not spent the time getting to know them, I would have been just another associate asking for my work to be done first. The other work in the queue was presumably just as important as what I was submitting, but the power of our relationship motivated them to help me.

Jamie and Ed were both up for promotion to executive vice president at Company X. Matt was one of the key people who would be making the promotion decision. Matt had worked with both Jamie and Ed, and thought that they were both strong professionals, with excellent skills and experiential portfolios. However, Matt had spent a significant amount of time with Jamie on three separate assignments and thought highly of her ability to diagnose a problem, develop solutions, and marshal resources around executing objectives. He felt they had a solid professional relationship and that he could give her honest, real-time feedback, when and if necessary.

The promotion would be a stretch assignment for both Jamie and Ed, but there needed to be absolute certainty around the candidate's ability to perform in the role. In the end, Matt supported Jamie's candidacy, who had the advantage because of their relationship and Matt's belief that if he supported her, she would follow his guidance and advice about how to be successful in the new position.

On the surface, Jamie and Ed were equally qualified for the job, but Matt's subjective judgment around potential future performance was influenced by the relationship that Jamie had established with him. Consider if Jamie had not invested in the relationship with Matt. Suppose she had approached her assignments with the mind-set of "I am just going to do my job and do it really well. I don't have time to worry about small talk or building relationships." Would Matt have felt as comfortable putting his support behind her? Perhaps someone else would have been more vocal on Ed's behalf. If Jamie had no other sponsorship, the job might have gone to Ed.

Relationship currency also gives you access to relationships you don't currently have. In large organizations, it is sometimes difficult to get exposure to very senior people or even to those who are just one to two levels above you. The easiest way to connect to people you don't know is to use or spend the currency that you have developed in a relationship to buy you access to a different one. If you have a good relationship with someone, they will often be willing to introduce you to others and even to use their reputation to vouch for you or to give you an endorsement. When introducing you to someone they know, people will often almost unconsciously say things like, "I'd like you to meet so and so, s/he and I go way back," or "s/he and I have worked together for a long time."

If you aren't present when someone is talking about you, they will say things like, "You should meet Olivia, she is good people," or, "I'll connect you with my friend/colleague, Olivia—you'll love her," or, "I think that you and Olivia will really hit it off." When you get that kind of endorsement, you have an opportunity to start a relationship that is already headed in a positive direction, not from anything that you did, but rather based on the other person's relationship to your colleague or friend making the introduction. This is powerful currency. It takes the goodwill and leverage that exists in one relationship and positively influences the trajectory of a new connection.

This is the premise behind the powerful company LinkedIn. The idea is to show all of the connections that any single person has and use those connections to create new relationships and networks. The concept is built upon the power of relationship currency to connect people. LinkedIn has grown from a small private company founded in 2002 to a multibillion-dollar public company with a projected growth rate in excess of 10 percent over the next few years.

Despite the obvious power of relationship currency, I have found many people reluctant to use this tool. Salespeople, financial advisors, and others have said to me, "I don't want to use my relationship with Person X (a client) to get access to Person Y. I feel like I am intruding on my relationship with Person X." No matter what your job, your friends, clients, and family can offer networks that can help you establish new relationships. And if you are really good at what you do, they are usually more than happy to make introductions for you. Take advantage of the strong reputation—the relationship currency—that you have with these constituencies. There is no better advantage to forming a new relationship than to begin it with a strong endorsement from someone who personally knows you.

You must remember, you have relationship currency because you've *earned* it. You have spent time getting to know someone, they like you, or you have somehow provided value to them or their endeavors. You're not going to lose the relationship because you attempt to use the currency you've earned to get exposure to another relationship.

The person you ask to make an introduction always has the power to say "no." And if that happens, you should graciously accept and respect that answer, and continue to move forward in your relationship. However, if they say "yes," then do your best to create a value-added experience for the person you will now have the chance to meet.

Sam was an entrepreneur and a major philanthropist in his community, and regularly gave of his time, talent, and money. He had been a weekly volunteer at the homeless shelter's food kitchen for the last eight years. He was a counselor at the Boys and Girls Club, ran every year in a marathon that raised funds for breast cancer research, and was a generous contributor to the local United Way. Sam was also a dedicated mentor to several young professionals in his community. There was someone Sam wanted to meet who could be instrumental in his next business venture, and this person happened to be a personal acquaintance of one of Sam's clients.

Sam was apprehensive about asking his client for the introduction, fearing that it might damage their good connection. After several attempts of trying to meet the person on his own, Sam decided to ask his client if he wouldn't mind brokering an introduction. Sam's client responded enthusiastically, "Sam, I would be more than happy to make the introduction. You have done so much for this community and for me personally. I have been wondering how I could show my gratitude for all that you have done for our neighborhood, and it would make me happy to do something for you." Sam was astounded. He never realized that his client was interested and willing to extend his relationship currency on his behalf. Like Sam, you may have people that you have helped or that you don't even know but who have observed you doing something and might just be waiting for a chance to repay you or do something on your behalf. If you have established a relationship with someone, a client, coworker, superior, friend, etc., recognize the currency you have earned with that person. Spend it as needed and allow the people who have currency with you to do the same.

If you have strong relationship currency, it can help you to recover when you make a mistake. There is generally no mistake that you can't recover from, *if* you have a strong relationship currency. If someone really trusts you and believes in your capabilities, they will generally give you another chance to continue to do business with them because of the strength of your relationship. If you do not have a strong relationship with someone and you make a mistake, they will likely move on to another provider of the service or the product or they will no longer have you as a member of their team.

I once priced a transaction that was set to open the next day. I was supposed to contact someone in our operations department to give them information that would allow them to release the stock in time for the stock exchange to open for the day's trading. If the stock did not open on time, it could cause it to trade in a way that would result in its decline in the open market and loss of money for my firm, which would have been a very bad outcome for the issuing company. Because the deal had a lot of complications and intricacies, I forgot to relay the information the night before as I should have. Early the next day, around 4:30 a.m., the operations person called to ask for the information, having realized my error. It's not the responsibility of the operations person to do this, but he did it because we had a good relationship. If he hadn't, there would have not been enough time to have the stock trade in an orderly fashion and it would have been squarely my fault—a disaster for me, the firm, and the client! Our relationship saved the day.

Imbalance of Trade in Relationships

One of the main ways I try to earn relationship currency in new connections is to create what I like to call "an imbalance of trade." It is a term I learned when I was new to the syndicate desk, and describes how much business each of the syndicate members do with each other on each deal that is executed in the public markets when one firm is a lead manager. In every public equity transaction there are a lead manager, comanagers, and syndicate members who are responsible for distributing the stock of a company when it is raising capital.

The lead manager changes from deal to deal, as do the syndicate members. Each underwriter keeps a record of how much they get paid as a lead manager and how much they are paid when they are syndicate members. Over time, you can detect a pattern when a certain firm is the lead manager and your firm is a syndicate member, and vice versa. For example, you can see that every time your firm is a lead manager, you pay a certain amount of money to a particular syndicate member. And when you are a syndicate member to their lead, your firm is paid substantially less. That is deemed to be an "imbalance of trade" that you would expect the other firm to balance out over time.

When I am approaching a new relationship, personally or professionally, I immediately start to think of ways that I can be helpful to the relationship. Notice I did not say I focus on what I can get. No, I ask myself: What can I do for them? How can I be helpful?

This is particularly the case in a client relationship. I listen intently to what they care about, what their challenges are, and what their specific issues might be. I start to think about how I could bring my intellect, problem-solving skills, experience, and firm resources to bear on the issue. Every time they need help, I offer to be of service, to find a way to be helpful. Over and over again, I try to invest in the relationship. In doing so, over time, we build a relationship and I create currency. The client may or may not give me firm business at the outset, but in the end, if I have effectively created currency in the relationship, I will have the ability to ask for the opportunity to compete the next time, and that *opportunity* is the first thing of value.

Later on, when I am once again competing for business, my relationship might turn out to be an advantage because the client trusts that I will make sure that the very best of my firm is delivered on their behalf. They know this because of my past behavior in our relationship when I delivered on my word and was of service to them, even when there was no deal or transaction at stake. I created an imbalance of trade that the client might seek to balance with a new deal at a later time.

Relationship Currency and Women

As we come to the end of our discussion on relationship and performance currency, I want to make an important distinction. While I don't often differentiate my advice between women and men, this is a point that I think is worth making. While women are very good in forming and sustaining relationships, I find that in corporate environments most women overinvest in performance currency relative to relationship currency.

In my opinion, male professionals start to invest in relationships very early on in their careers, almost simultaneously as they are creating performance currency. Alternatively, I have observed that women professionals tend to focus more on performance currency sometimes to the exclusion of investing in relationship currency. Women want to make sure that the work is stellar, even beyond reproach and that they cannot be criticized on the delivery of the work product. Over time, women continue to focus on the performance and do not invest time into building relationships. I believe that this could be a contributing factor as to why men have traditionally moved ahead a little faster than women.

Who knows you? Who trusts your work? Who believes that you have excellent judgment, and that you can manage and inspire people? Who feels like they know you well enough to consider you to be one of their partners?

If you are a female professional, I urge you to divert some of your energies away from performance currency and start investing in the key relationships in your environment. I am not saying that you can abandon your efforts to put points on the board, because without them you won't be able to move ahead. What I *am* saying is that you should start to focus on building relationships and earning relationship currency as soon as possible. Certainly, if you're a senior-level woman who has been with a company for a long period of time and are trying to move to the next level, you'll have to focus disproportionately on building relationship currency. Your currency as a performer has already been established in the organization and offers you diminishing marginal returns at this stage of your career. Your upside is in creating stronger relationship currency.

◄ *Carla's Pearls* ►

1. Relationship currency is very different from performance currency. Relationships are a medium of
   exchange you can use to further your professional
   agenda; acquire more responsibility, more senior
   roles, and greater assignments; and have your voice
   heard.
2. Begin to build relationships as soon as you join an
   organization. Create a broad network of those senior to you, junior to you, and peers.
3. You create relationship currency by making the
   time and effort to connect with people over business and personal topics. Be deliberate about connecting with people: put it as an action item on your
   calendar if necessary.
4. True relationship currency will motivate people to
   act on your behalf.
5. Women must be sure to focus on relationship currency as much as, if not more than, performance
   currency.

CHAPTER 6

Effective Communication and Reading the Signs

"The most important thing about communicating is hearing what isn't said."

—Peter Drucker

In my experience, it is rarely someone's ability or work ethic that holds them back, but rather, people's careers often stall because they don't know how to effectively communicate. Good communication has two components. The first is the ability to effectively communicate with colleagues—how well you articulate (verbally and in writing) who you are, what you can do, and what you want from your career. It includes your skill in asking questions and for help when you need it, as well as your ability to say "no" to someone more senior than you.

The second part of good communication involves listening, but not simply to what is being said verbally. How well do you understand and respond appropriately to what is *not* being said? Can you decipher signs being given by your organization or the implications made by your bosses in both informal and formal conversations (such as evaluation and feedback sessions)? The ability to listen and read the signs is a vital skill for success.

Effective Communication

For the first time in the history of corporate America, we have a multigenerational environment, and awareness of this is crucial. Four distinct generations—Traditionalists (those born before 1946), Baby Boomers (born 1946–1964), Generation Xers (1965–1980), and Millennials (born 1981–2000) are productively working together in the same environments. In general, each group has a unique communication style. Understanding those differing styles can be a useful and important tool in helping you effectively communicate with your colleagues.

Consider the Millennials. They are comfortable sending e-mails and texts to communicate with others. In fact, they place the same level of importance on face-to-face meetings as they do on a text message. However, this is not generally the case for the Baby Boomers. For them, face-to-face meetings have more weight and are considered far more important than text messages or e-mails.

I want to make an important point here. It should go without saying that you should use correct grammar when writing or speaking. But in these days of "LOL," "TY," "OMG," and other smartphone and Internet slang, I think it is worth stating. Using poor grammar, colloquialisms, misspellings, or abbreviations as you would in a text message to a friend is the easiest way to appear unprofessional, lose your listener in a meeting or presentation, or the reader of your memo or e-mail. These poor habits are distracting and cause people to focus on your mistakes rather than whatever message you are attempting to communicate.

People who are successful communicators don't just focus on the message they want to deliver, they also consider the receiver and their preferences. If your boss is a Baby Boomer, a face-to-face meeting when you have an important message to share would likely be far more effective than sending a text or e-mail. If your boss is in the office next to yours, don't e-mail them! Get up from your desk, knock on the door, and poke your head in and have a conversation. If, on the other hand, you know your boss has a preference for e-mail communication, then by all means, e-mail it is.

In addition, while we are all addicted to checking our smartphones, reading e-mails or text messages while you are in a work meeting is rude. I constantly see young professionals make this mistake. I even once heard of a job candidate taking a phone call in the middle of an interview! Needless to say, he didn't get the job. If a colleague, or more important a senior person, is talking in a meeting or conversation and pauses, that is not an opportunity for you to look at your smartphone. You may not be talking, but your nonverbal communication is sending the message that you are not paying attention. This is a quick way to damage your relationship currency as well as others' perception of you.

If you are in a conversation with someone, look at them while they are talking, engage actively, and respond accordingly until the conversation is over. This is true particularly if the person you are speaking to is a Boomer or Traditionalist. Remember, what you say is only half of the effective communication equation; the other half requires making sure the person you are communicating with is fully receiving your message.

Speaking with clarity and impact is saying what you want to say in a way that your listener will hear it, embrace it, and act upon it in the way you want them to. For example, if you would like a raise, you could go in to your boss and say, "I think I deserve a raise and I would like to get one," but a better approach would be to say something like, "I would like to be considered for a raise this year for the following three reasons: I have been a major contributor to the three most important projects that our department has had, which have resulted in X thousands of dollars for the company; I have been active and successful in recruiting Y new people to the company, which was one of our most important objectives this year; and I have helped the firm save Z thousands of dollars this year with our expense reduction program."

While both examples of communication are direct, the second one gives your boss a very clear idea of why you are approaching him or her for a raise and your justification for the request. The second example will be more seriously considered because it is delivered in person in a clear, concise, thoughtful manner, and is a sound argument, versus the first example, which, while direct, offers no justification or rationale.

Especially when you are speaking to someone who is more senior to you, work to be direct and concise in your communication. That does not mean that you should be incomplete in your rationale or in your thoughts, but rather, you should avoid extra explanations that go beyond your direct request or statement. If you're meeting with your boss to discuss a project you've been working on, go in prepared to talk about the goals of the assignment, any changes to them during the process, and the outcome. Show how you got there, what processes you used, or the assumptions made in your original analysis. Then be sure to pause and ask for any questions or observations. Answer them if necessary and then continue your discussion from there.

While addressing these things is important, I'll caution you not to get bogged down in superfluous details, especially as a way of showing how smart you are. For example, it's not necessary to detail why you chose these assumptions yet rejected the four others you could have made, or why you chose this methodology and not the other two that you could have used. Bosses generally want the answer. If they are interested in other ways that you could have done the analysis, they will ask. This was an interesting lesson for me to learn. Early in my career, I was anxious to demonstrate how smart I was and how thorough I had been in conducting a piece of analysis that was assigned to me. When it was time for the team to present to the boss, I insisted that I be the person to do so, as I had done a lot of the work to produce the conclusion.

As I began, I went into all the background behind the analysis, how long it had taken to gather the information, all the sources that we used to derive the answers, the problems that we encountered with the data, and so on. I had been speaking for about fifteen minutes when the boss finally interrupted and said, "For Pete's sake, what's the answer?"

I was so stunned I could barely speak! At the time, I had no idea why he responded that way. Didn't he want to know how thorough I had been? Didn't I need to justify why I had chosen the methodology and the assumptions I used? Wasn't that a demonstration of my intellect? While the outcome that I presented was the one he was hoping for, I had not impressed him with my delivery. I had lost almost all of the value of the hard work that I had done by giving too detailed information.

If I had presented using the focused, streamlined approach, I would have not only gotten credit for the great answer, but my boss would have perceived me as a sharp, smart associate who had good judgment about what was important to present and about the use of his time. I would have probably earned the opportunity to work with him again soon. In reality, I did not get an opportunity to work for him for a long time and missed the chance to work on a few really great transactions. What you say and how you say it has implications for how you are perceived in your environment and we know that perceptions directly impact your ability to ascend in an organization.

Emotions in Your Communications

If you read *Expect to Win*, you know that I am big fan of you being your authentic self and that I believe emotions are a natural part of who we are as humans. However, it is important to discern what parts of your authentic self should be exhibited and when. Bringing all of who you are to work, at all times (particularly if you tend to be an emotionally expressive person) is not a good idea. While we all get upset at work from time to time, demonstrative displays of extreme emotions in your communications at work should be avoided. Yelling at coworkers or your boss, hysterically crying when you are upset, slamming drawers or doors, storming out of offices, and other similar behaviors are all off limits in the workplace.

While something may happen that makes you feel that these behaviors might be justified, keep in mind that it is difficult to recover your professional reputation and continue to move ahead in your career once you have had an outburst like this. When things do happen that are adverse in your environment, and chances are at some point they will, approach the situation by maintaining a calm and professional demeanor. You will receive a lot of credit and admiration, or even gain currency in your environment, because of how well you handled the situation.

You should feel comfortable expressing normal emotions in your office environment. If someone tells a joke that is funny, obviously you should laugh. If something negative happens, like the passing away of a colleague's parent or spouse, you can certainly show sorrow, disappointment, or surprise. The way that you should communicate should be authentic to who you are, and if you have chosen an environment and culture that is consistent with who you are, then the way that you communicate will be accepted by others in your company.

One of the easiest ways to tell if you are being too emotional is to listen closely for your use of the pronoun "I." If you hear yourself saying things like, "I think," "I feel," "I," "I," "I," then stop and review whether you are being emotional or taking a stance that is all about you. While you should be focused on managing your career and getting ahead, remember you have to do that in the context of your work environment. Unless you have clear evidence to the contrary, approach your career platform with the attitude that "what is good for the team will directly benefit me."

This is not to say that you shouldn't take credit for the things that you accomplish; you certainly should. But you can do so and still demonstrate a team-oriented focus. None of us can operate effectively alone in the workplace. We all need other relationships. I cannot think of one industry, or one role within an industry, that is not somehow interdependent upon someone else in that company or environment.

When you are leading a team, it is important that you use the pronoun "we" far more often than the pronoun "I," especially when you are communicating about accomplishments. Giving credit to your team for the accomplishments that the group makes, and even the accomplishment that you make as a member of the team, will create more relationship currency for you within your team and within your company. Saying "we" rather than "I" will generate greater credibility for you as a leader, not less. It is clear to the organization that the team could not have accomplished what it did without a good leader, so by extension you will personally get credit within the organization. But more important, you will engender trust and loyalty from your team members and they will want to work with and for you even more. This applies even when you are not leading the team.

If you are having a team discussion and you disagree with a coworker or your boss, you should feel comfortable expressing your dissenting opinion. But the key to building currency, as opposed to damaging it, is *how* you express that opinion. In expressing emotion, be conscious of and understand your overall environment and the culture, and express yourself in a way that is consistent with how people speak to one another effectively.

For example, if one colleague disagrees with another and the culture is a very open, direct, and aggressive one, the dissenting opinion might be expressed as follows: "John, that answer makes no sense." Alternatively, in a culture that is more genteel or team-oriented, the opinion might be expressed in this way: "John, that is an interesting thought. Allow me to push back on that for a second." Both responses are expressing an opposing sentiment, but each is expressed differently and consistent with what is accepted in that culture. If the first answer was given in the second culture, it would have been disruptive to the meeting and likely not embraced or absorbed by those who were participating in the meeting. If the second answer had been offered in the first culture, it may have been overlooked and ignored.

When you have an answer or an opinion that is different from your team, your coworkers, or your boss, it is important that you listen closely and completely to what they have to say. Wait until they have finished before you offer your thoughts. You should begin your communication by acknowledging that you've heard what they had to say, but there is something that you would like to communicate in addition to their thoughts, saying something like this: "I heard your point clearly, especially the point about X, but I would like to add this thought and get your thoughts about this fact or about this point." Then you should pause and give them an opportunity to react or respond. You should then offer your additional thoughts about why you think the point is a good one. If it is a point that you feel strongly about, then you should offer up the opportunity to provide additional data or research and set up a time to discuss the point further at a later time.

Suppose someone in your environment asks you to do additional work, but you don't believe that you can get it done effectively with your current workload. It's important that you can communicate "no" in a way that includes a clear explanation of why you don't think you will be able to perform the task well.

Again, saying "no" is not the issue; the effectiveness of your response is in *how* you say "no" and the rationale that you provide. Saying "Tom, I am so busy. Why does everyone keep dumping all of the work on me!" won't go over very well. But "Tom, I would love to take on that assignment, but I have something due tomorrow for Ron and then three deliverables by Friday, so I don't think that I will be able to execute the project fully" will be much better received.

If you are working for more than one person at once, then you should always communicate your current workload to whoever is asking you to work on something. If the person suggests that the project they are asking you to work on has a greater priority than the others you are working on, then you should suggest that the three of you get in a room, or at the very least have a quick conference call or group e-mail to agree on priorities.

Never let your desire to please someone cause you to ultimately disappoint someone else and thereby impair your performance currency. To avoid this, you must communicate the potential conflict early and effectively. How and to whom you communicate is of paramount importance to your ability to be successful at work, particularly when you are communicating a "no" or disappointing message.

Receiving the All-Important Performance Review—and Other Feedback Communication

Some of the most difficult communications that you will be involved in at work will be around feedback on your performance. There are two things that are important about this kind of communication: 1) whether it is verbal or nonverbal; and 2) how you respond to that communication.

One of the most common disappointments I hear about from people with career issues is about the promotion they didn't get.

What's more striking is that they were usually completely surprised by it, either because: 1) while they had not previously had a conversation about it, they expected that the organization would just naturally promote them when they had reached a certain level of seniority; or 2) the feedback communication loop had not been clear and distinct and/or they failed to understand the signs and the messages that were indicating that no promotion was coming.

Most companies have human resources departments that develop and implement performance reviews that offer employees feedback on how they have executed the requirements of their job throughout the year and identify developmental needs. The underlying assumption inherent in the review process is that the information discovered during the evaluation will be delivered in a constructive and clear manner, allowing each employee to clearly understand what they are executing well, what they need to improve, and any skills that they need to acquire in order to continue moving up in the organization or along their career journey.

Unfortunately, the reality is that in many cases these messages are either not delivered effectively or they are not delivered at all. Information is conveyed to the employee in an unclear or unhelpful manner that doesn't give them guidance on how to improve or doesn't adequately communicate information about their career trajectory.

Most organizations have nonconfrontational cultures where human resources professionals counsel and train managers to avoid giving employees feedback in a way that might upset, disillusion, or worse, provoke an employee to pursue litigation against the company.

Unfortunately, as a result, even when there is a serious performance issue, feedback is often delivered using such carefully constructed language that the real message about what someone needs to do to improve or change is diluted. This does the employee a real disservice, as they likely don't understand that they have a developmental need or that their performance is not up to par with the company's expectations and as a result can impact their career progression.

Michael worked for five years as an accounts payable clerk and wanted to be promoted to manager. In his last performance review, Michael was told that he was "doing a good job and to keep up the good work." As a result, he assumed that he was on track to be promoted. However, during his discussion with his boss, there was no mention of a potential promotion next year. Further, there was no conversation about the kinds of skills and experiences that one needed to be considered for promotion.

Over the course of the year, Michael noticed that some of his contemporaries were being asked to work on more project-oriented assignments that involved managing small teams of people. He did not worry about it, because he had plenty of assignments of his own. In fact, he was getting more and more of the same type of work he had become skilled at (because his colleagues were focused on their special assignments). Michael assumed that since he was successfully completing the work and there were no complaints about his efforts that all was well and he was on track for a promotion. After all, he had been there for five years. It was time, wasn't it?

At the end of the year, Michael did not get promoted, but two of his colleagues did. Feeling unfairly treated, he was crushed, disillusioned, and wanted to leave the company. What Michael failed to recognize was that despite the "doing a good job" feedback he had received, there was a message in the fact that he continued to get the same kind of work while his colleagues were working on different, project-management-oriented assignments showcasing their potential and skills as managers.

When he had his performance review, Michael should have

asked questions about his work assignments and articulated his expectations about getting promoted. If nothing else, he would have provoked a conversation about his prospects and would have had a better understanding of whether the organization was thinking of him as a management candidate. In this case, it was not what was said in Michael's feedback communication, but rather what was not mentioned. The fact that a promotion opportunity never came up in the conversation should have been a signal to Michael to ask about it.

When going into any performance feedback meeting, be prepared with a clear view of how you think you have performed in that year, in that quarter, or on particular assignments. Know what you did really well and what you think you could have done differently or improved. If you made a mistake during a project, be specific as to why you think you made the mistake and what you would do differently if given the opportunity to try again. Remember, it is important to show that you take some responsibility for any mistake even if others contributed to it.

If you have a strong assessment of yourself and your abilities when walking into the meeting, then you will be able to easily compare and contrast the feedback that is communicated to you. Calmly absorb the information you hear and then say, "I'd like to respond to a couple of the points that you communicated and discuss them further." Then you can ask specifically about the things that were communicated that were in direct contrast to your expectations. Again, you should communicate in a way that is measured, clear, concise, and nonemotional. You want to send the message that you are open to what is being said and seeking to understand the communication, absorb it, and act upon it. State this definitively and allow your body language (your nonverbal communication) to support it.

If you have been having frequent and active communications at work, then what you hear in a feedback session should never be a surprise. Having regular conversations with your boss and colleagues along the way about the projects that you are working on will prevent issues later. After a project is complete, routinely say "I think that this project went well. In particular, I thought that we did the following two or three things really well. I wish I had an opportunity to do X again. I think we might have improved on that. What are your thoughts about the project?"

When you receive feedback, be absolutely sure that you clearly understand what is being communicated to you. If you are at all unclear about the message, ask questions. For example, suppose your manager tells you that your analytical skills are "not where they should be at this stage of your career." Your response should be, "Can you give me a few examples? I am familiar with the models that we use and have not made any mistakes on my assignments. What do you believe is prompting this feedback?" If your boss says to you, "We don't believe you are quite ready for a promotion," your response should be, "That is disappointing to hear. Can you tell me specifically what I should do in the next year to make me an attractive candidate for promotion?"

In almost every feedback conversation, you can expect both verbal and nonverbal communications. You should play close attention to what is being said to you and what is not being communicated verbally. Never leave a feedback conversation feeling any ambiguity about the message you received.

Reading the Signs—Hearing What Is Not Being Said

When you are not receiving challenging assignments that give you an opportunity to prove yourself in new ways, you should start to pay close attention to what messages your company or your manager may be sending. Doing similar tasks for a year or even two, especially in a tough economic environment, is common. However, when there is no mention about changing your tasks or giving you more responsibility by year two, then either the organization has tapped out on career mobility options for you, or management is sending you a signal that they are not sure that you are capable of taking on expanded responsibilities or more challenging assignments. This means that your career at the company could be stalling, or worse, that you have been identified as someone who is expendable if a further economic downturn occurs.

You might be asking yourself, "Why wouldn't my boss just come straight out and say what the issues are about my performance? If someone just told me what to do, I could do it." While many companies have a well-defined feedback communication policy and they can and do clearly communicate expectations about tasks, the actual responsibility for feedback about day-to-day duties is assigned to individual managers and departments. Some managers are not comfortable communicating feedback, especially when it involves criticism. Ultimately, this means that while your company may have a well-developed human resources feedback and developmental mechanism (such as the formal review), your opportunity to receive clear, developmental feedback will depend upon what department you are working in and who is communicating that feedback to you. Because this all happens at the "local" level, that feedback could be, and often is, inconsistent with the company's standard processes.

In addition, as we discussed, many companies are extremely careful in giving feedback. No one wants an employee to get upset, cause a ruckus, or incite other negative reactions from other professionals (or worse, file a suit against the company for unfair treatment). If the person responsible for giving you feedback thinks you might react negatively, they are likely to water down the message.

The problem with this approach is that you may leave a feedback session without a clear understanding of what you need to improve or whether you need to invest in further training to enhance your position in the company. In addition, sometimes the feedback a manager or other leader wants to give you is personal and falls outside the confines of what is permissible for a company to communicate. Generally the feedback that a company is allowed to give must relate to the defined performance criteria for your particular job, department, and company. Technically, the evaluation of your performance is about how you execute and deliver.

At the local level, however, it is not uncommon for people to have judgments about you as a person, how you dress, the way you wear your hair, and even about your presentation style. These subjective judgments can affect the feedback you receive and your ability to move up within the organization. And because this kind of feedback generally cannot be communicated in a formal review session, you may never hear some of these things.

It's up to you to watch for the signals. For example, if someone thinks that you dress unprofessionally, or at least in a way considered inappropriate for meeting clients, they may never mention it formally. But what they might do is simply not invite you to client meetings. If someone does not think that you will present to clients in a cogent, concise, compelling manner, they might invite you to a meeting, but won't give you a speaking role. While it would be helpful for your boss to give you honest, direct feedback, the truth is, for all of the reasons just enumerated, they often won't. It is incumbent upon you to be aware of the trends, to read the signals, and to respond accordingly by asking for clarity around these issues.

Kelly really wanted a promotion. She was certain she had

done everything she needed to do to earn one, yet for the last
two years she had been passed over. Kelly's mentor advised her to
sit down with her boss and articulate her desire for a promotion
and find out specifically what was keeping it from happening.
Kelly followed that advice and arranged a meeting.

During the discussion she received very ambiguous feedback. In response, she probed after every piece of feedback she
was given. For example, her boss mentioned that she did not
have "gravitas" with clients and Kelly asked what she was doing
to create that impression when she had a track record of giving
very tough advice to her clients that they followed. If she did
not have gravitas, her clients would have questioned her advice,
potentially gone over her head to seek her boss's advice, or perhaps changed advisors. In fact, her clients had complimented
her for having the courage to give them the tough advice.

Her boss mentioned that there was feedback questioning
her analytical capabilities and she asked for specific examples
where she had failed to demonstrate her expertise. He could not
give her specific examples. She left the meeting concluding that
her boss either did not have the internal political clout to secure
a promotion for her, or worse, that he was holding her back because he himself was not moving forward.

After the conversation with her boss, Kelly had another
meeting with her mentor and shared what had taken place. Kelly's mentor confirmed for her that her performance was fine but
that she had poor relationship currency with her boss, who had
poor political currency in the environment. Kelly's mentor advised her to work to expand the support for her promotion by
developing a relationship with her boss's boss and others in the
department.

Kelly was terrified that her boss would be angry about her
building relationships with others, especially his boss. But Kelly's mentor assured her that as a professional in the organization,

developing relationships with people at all levels was important and that her boss should not block her ability to do that. Second, the mentor explained that it was critical to get other support because her inability to get promoted was not performance related, and that her boss did not have enough political clout to get her promoted without the support of others more senior to him and displayed a nonchalant attitude toward her moving ahead.

If you have had a conversation with a boss or peer, received confusing feedback, and asked clarifying questions but still are unclear, your mentor is the perfect place to turn to help you decipher what was communicated. They can help you figure out both the verbal and nonverbal messages and make sure your action plan is consistent with what you need to do to move forward.

If Kelly had not had the conversation with her mentor, she may not have really understood why she wasn't getting promoted and may have embarked on the wrong path to move forward toward the promotion she wanted.

But Kelly was scared to execute the plan her mentor suggested. She sat for another year without taking any action and still didn't get promoted. She was devastated. She spent five years as a vice president, while her peers were generally promoted within three. Finally, Kelly started to realize that she had nothing to lose in taking the risk to execute the plan her mentor had suggested a year before. She was so unhappy in her current position she knew she would eventually leave anyway if something didn't change. The worst that could happen was that her boss would admonish her for developing other internal relationships and continue not supporting her promotion. On the other hand, she reasoned, if she could expose other people to her work, she might be able to generate support and ultimately find another sponsor and get promoted.

Kelly began to have a quarterly meeting about her work and other departmental initiatives with her boss's boss. She made sure to invite him along with her boss to client events that she organized. He quickly started to see for himself what an asset she was to the department. The very next review cycle, Kelly received her promotion.

Since Kelly's boss could not give her concrete feedback about her performance, she should have read the signal that her failure to get promoted was not about her contributions but rather about something else. If she had executed on her mentor's advice sooner she would have been promoted a year earlier.

If you are having trouble recognizing and deciphering the signs in your environment, then discuss your observations with a mentor or trusted friend. In some cases, it might be appropriate to approach the person you think is sending a message and ask directly if they are trying to tell you something. That can help clarify whether what you think you see is true or if you are being overly sensitive.

I once worked with an officer who clearly respected my work, but would never allow me to speak in a client meeting. I would work on the project, prepare the analysis for the presentation, and be invited to the meeting. But he would do the entire presentation himself and I would only get to speak if there was a specific question about one of the assumptions in the analysis.

After having a conversation with my peers about their experiences, I learned that they were presenting at least a small portion of the presentation they had prepared for clients. I decided to approach the officer directly about it. I said, "Is there an opportunity for me to present in our next client meeting? I would really like to be able to get that experience." The officer hesitated and then finally said, "Carla, I think sometimes you can be a little verbose, and I don't want you to go on too long in front of the client. That's one of the reasons that I haven't had you present so far." I then said to him, "Okay I understand, but how about I come to your office and give you a preview of what

I will say in the meeting and then you can tell me if it's good or if I need to refine it. Then let's give it a chance." He agreed and I presented in the next meeting.

I read the signal that he was reticent about my presentation skills. I was confident that he thought I was smart and that my work was good because of the positive communication that he gave me around my analysis and the fact that he kept inviting me to client meetings, but the lack of invitations to present suggested there was something else at play, too. It was my responsibility to find out what it was. The important thing is that I stepped up, asked the question, and communicated it in a way that he didn't feel threatened to discuss it.

When a professional is repeatedly passed over for promotion or not being offered new assignments or other opportunities for development, the organization is usually sending the person a signal. Usually, the company is hoping the person will be satisfied in the role they are in, or get the message and move on.

But never assume. If you are interested in more responsibility or a promotion, and you aren't getting it, exercise your power and ask why. You may very well be surprised by the answer.

A young lady, Kita, approached me about this topic following one of my speaking engagements. She had been with her company for a long time and had received positive feedback each year during evaluations, but she had never had a conversation with her boss about promotions.

I asked her, "Have you asked your boss about promotion opportunities and expressed interest in ascending in the organization?" Her answer was all too common. "Doesn't he know that I want to move ahead?" she said. As I've said, it is not your boss's responsibility to think about when you should be promoted or to assume that you are interested in a promotion.

Some people are perfectly happy to get into a stable role that they think offers some job security and allows them a certain standard of living. And no one assumes that anyone is necessarily seeking to move ahead. After our discussion, Kita went to her boss and expressed an interest in being promoted. He told her that he had no idea that she was interested in a different role. During the next promotion cycle, she was promoted to a new position.

Signals are important and the ability to read and decipher them is a vital skill that will help you move forward in your career. If you believe you are getting signals but don't understand them, consider asking a mentor, sponsor, or your boss the following questions, which can help you decipher the signs and understand what is really going on with your career trajectory. The following scenarios might help you identify and interpret situations you could encounter in your career.

Scenario #1

Cole is a plant manager for a consumer products company and has risen through the ranks to supervisor. The company is doing well, is expanding its product line, and is focused on accelerating sales. The division's vice president has said the company is specifically looking to hire sales professionals who have previous experience with the company's products and the ability to articulate the company's strengths.

In April, Cole's boss approached him about taking on the sales position. Cole declined the offer because he did not feel he could be successful. He had no previous sales experience and did not want to set himself up to fail. He felt secure in his position as plant manager and wanted to stay there.

In September, Cole received his evaluation and was told that he had done exceptionally well and that the company thought that he had great management abilities. His boss also told him that he thought Cole was ready for a new challenge and repeated his recommendation that Cole consider taking on one of the new sales roles. Cole thanked his boss for the positive comments, but reiterated his satisfaction with his plant manager position.

The next month, Cole's boss formally approached him again, asking him to consider the sales role, which was entering the final stage of the hiring process. Cole once again declined, thinking, "Whenever there is a downturn of any kind in the economy or the business, the salespeople are the first to go." In December, the company announced that they were restructuring plant operations and implementing a new automated system that would significantly reduce production costs, but also meant layoffs. Cole was offered a severance package.

Cole's boss obviously had known about the company's plans to restructure its operations. However, he could not share this confidential information with Cole, who, unfortunately, failed to read the signals he was being sent. Cole's mistake was focusing on all the potential downside risks of trying something new without even considering that there might be a good reason his boss was strongly urging him to look at new opportunities. Even after his boss approached him formally twice and offered him a new opportunity, he still thought that he had a choice to decline.

At a minimum, Cole should have asked questions like, Is this just a polite suggestion, or do you think considering this change would be in my best interests? Why specifically do you think that I will be good in a sales position? What are the future opportunities if I move into a sales role versus staying in an operations function? Does the company have any plans to change or restructure current plant operations? The answers to any of these questions might have signaled to Cole that his boss wasn't suggesting, but rather strongly recommending he take the next step in his career.

When your boss is making specific suggestions to you about new positions, or stretch assignments, you should read that as a positive signal that your boss and the organization view you as a strong team player and someone they would like to keep and promote. Your boss would not be making suggestions to you about trying new things if you have not been identified as someone who is a leader in the environment. Even if they are thinking about restructuring and may not be thinking of promoting you at this time, the fact that they are making suggestions about your taking on new assignments or roles generally means that they are trying to put you in a secure spot while the company continues to make other changes in the organization.

Scenario #2

Jackie had a goal of becoming a senior officer at the telecommunications company where she worked by the time she was forty years old. Having reached the milestone on her last birthday, she felt compelled to apply for an opening for a senior vice president of operations that had recently been posted. She approached her boss, Barbara, and asked for her support in getting the promotion. Barbara told her that because she only recently was promoted to vice president, she was not eligible to compete for the role. She also reminded her that there were several other, more senior candidates in the queue for the job. Barbara told Jackie that she was doing a stellar job, was a highly valued member of the team, and was someone that the company was looking at for future leadership opportunities.

Despite this, Jackie went ahead and applied. She felt that if she didn't get this promotion she would need to leave the company and find an officer role elsewhere. After several interviews, Jackie learned she did not get the position, but that she was "very close in the process" and likely to get the next officer role that became available. Despite this, Jackie felt the company did not value her and started preparing to leave.

In this case, Jackie completely missed the signals that the company valued her and would make her a senior officer in due time: 1) the company allowed her to compete for the senior role; 2) her manager, Barbara, went out of her way to communicate to Jackie that he she was valued by the company; 3) Jackie was given definitive feedback after the process that she had prospective opportunities.

If Jackie had had another conversation with Barbara after not being chosen for the position, she would have been encouraged to continue on the course that she was on with the company instead of interrupting her career trajectory to move to another organization when her performance and relationship currency were strong at her old firm.

Scenario #3

Clare's boss, Karen, is up for promotion to managing director of an investment bank. She is nervous about getting the job and focused on making sure her team produces the best work possible. She has given Clare an assignment, but she is constantly checking in to make sure that it is on track. It has been a week since Clare received the assignment, which is due the next day.

Clare turned in part of the assignment to Karen. She took it upon herself to complete the task in a new way, believing the way she conducted the analysis to be better than the methodology her boss preferred. Having used it to execute other assignments, Clare was sure this was the best approach. When Karen realized what Clare did, she got angry and chewed Clare out in front of the team, demanding that she redo the analysis work in the way she prefers. Now Clare believes her boss thinks she isn't competent, doesn't like her, and is being unfair.

What Clare has failed to realize is that her boss is feeling insecure and nervous about a potential big promotion. As such, it was not the right time to introduce a new way of executing assignments and expect to get the boss's sign-off. Clare's boss wants to make sure that all the work coming from the team is consistent with what she normally produces, with no surprises or errors. She does not want to take a chance that any assignment could derail her from receiving the promotion. This situation has nothing to do with Clare and whether or not she is good at her job, but everything to do with her introducing an unknown into the situation during a time when her boss wants to play it safe. Clare has failed to read the situation correctly with respect to her boss's mind-set.

Scenario #4

George had been in his current position for seven years. During every evaluation cycle he got feedback that he was doing a great job, and should keep doing what he was doing. In addition, every time new people joined the team, George was asked to train them during their three-month probationary period. Many of the people he had trained had moved on to other areas of the company to become supervisors. In addition, at least four opportunities for new managers had been posted within George's department, and each time the company brought in someone from the outside or promoted someone at his level from another office to take the position instead of him.

George didn't know what to think about this. If he was doing a good job, why wasn't he ever offered the promotion? There were a number of possibilities. The senior people and decision makers may not see George as a potential manager. Or they didn't think he aspired to be a manager and was happy in his current position. Perhaps George lacked the credentials the company required for employees to become managers, so therefore despite his experience George was ineligible for a promotion. Maybe George was simply being overlooked.

How should he interpret this situation? How should he handle it? No matter how he looked at the situation, the potential reasons he hadn't been promoted were all poor reasons. It was time for George to have a few direct conversations with his boss, mentors, and other people of influence at his workplace. First, he needed to understand the criteria that made someone eligible to run the office and he should directly ask his boss this question. Second, he needed to figure out what perception the decision makers had about him by speaking to his mentors and peers. And finally, he needed to express an interest in managing the office and throw his hat into the ring for consideration the next time an opportunity became available.

George sat down to talk to his boss, Marty.

"Marty, I would love to understand the criteria that are used for promoting someone to the manager role in the office." After Marty explained the criteria, George should say, "Thanks very much for sharing that with me. I would like to express that I am very interested in being promoted to a manager. I have been with the firm for seven years and have significant experience in training and motivating several rounds of new employees, many of whom have gone on to more senior positions. I think that I can play an important role in training and developing the professionals for this office, enhancing our productivity and preparing leaders for other parts of the company. How can I make sure that I am seriously considered the next time a managerial opportunity arises?"

If Marty responds by telling George that he would make sure he is considered the next time a manager position becomes available, then George's problem is solved. But on the other hand, if Marty expresses reservations about his candidacy, George should explore the reasons why. If his boss says George needs a degree, a certain amount of time in a position, or some other certification, then George should express his intention to acquire the necessary degree or certificate and reiterate his interest and intention in pursuing the promotion.

Here are some common signals and examples of the questions you might ask in order to clarify what these signals mean:

Signal #1: Presentation skills are valued in your department, but you are never given an opportunity to present in front of clients.

Questions: Can you give me a sense of how my presentation skills are viewed? What should I do to improve them? Are there other opportunities for me to present internally so that people (decision makers) can be exposed to my capabilities? May I have a small portion of the presentation to present to the client in our next meeting?

Signal #2: You are assigned small sales accounts and never have an opportunity to go after larger accounts.

Questions: The accounts that I am given seem to have limited growth potential. I have done an analysis, and at best there is 10–20 percent upside with these accounts in the next twelve months. As I am interested in obtaining greater exposure to larger compensation opportunities, I would like to have a shot at some of the larger, more complex accounts. Can you tell me what I need to do to be eligible for that kind of assignment?

Signal #3: Because one assignment did not go particularly well, you have received feedback that you are not an effective manager. Since then you have not been given an opportunity to manage a large group of people, and management skills are a prerequisite for the next promotion. You should seek to understand if this is a signal that you will never get an opportunity for promotion because of this one experience or if it's feedback that is specific to this one assignment.

Questions: I understand that my last managerial experience was not a particularly good one. After much reflection and considering the feedback you gave me, I understand the mistakes that I made. I would like an opportunity to demonstrate that I have absorbed your feedback and can execute the suggestions and remedies offered. Is there a project where I could manage a team and demonstrate my readiness to take on larger managerial opportunities since that is a skill necessary for me to ascend in the organization?

While most organizations place a premium on strong communication skills, important data and information is shared through nonverbal signals. Unfortunately, many bright, capable professionals miss the messages being communicated to them, both the positive and the negative, and therefore miss opportunities to advance, to correct an action, or even to leave a company before it is too late.

As I like to say, "You can't fix it if you don't know that it's broken." Whether the signals are good or bad, asking questions and listening carefully to the answers will help you understand the situation better and determine what to do in response to keep your career moving forward. And keep in mind, whatever your role, you should always create an environment where people, no matter who they are or what their title, can feel comfortable giving you feedback. Whether or not you think it is valid, never be argumentative or aggressive toward someone offering you constructive criticism. Instead, take it in, make sure you have a clear understanding of what is being said—and not said. This is a key skill that will help you continue to grow and successfully move forward in your career.

◄ Carla's Pearls ►

1. Ineffective communication skills can be a major impediment to moving ahead and maximizing your success. There are different ways to communicate to your boss, your peers, and people who are junior to you.

2. Do not be too emotional in your communication at work, stay professional.

3. Much of the feedback that you receive can be non-verbal. Many professionals miss the messages being communicated to them, both the positive and negative, and therefore miss opportunities to advance, to correct an action, or even to leave a company before it is too late. It is up to you to watch for the signals and ask the questions necessary to have a clear picture of how you are perceived and whether your performance is up to par.

4. Know the common signals and ask questions about what they mean, and adjust your performance as necessary to keep your career moving forward.

5. You can't fix it if you don't know that it's broken. Whether or not you think it is valid, never be argumentative or aggressive toward someone offering you constructive criticism. Be open to what people have to communicate: it will help you continue to grow.

CHAPTER 7

Positioning Your Profile for Success in the Professional Environment

"Man, know thyself."

—Socrates

Each of us has a profile at work. One of the most important facets of positioning yourself for success is to be self-aware. You must know who you are and who you aspire to be. I find that many professionals do not proceed successfully in their career because they are not aware of who they really are, how they manifest themselves at work, and how their work profile is or is not consistent with what is valued in the organization or with the current economic environment. The profile is the way your colleagues, including your peers and those senior to you, would describe how you fit into the organization. Your profile is very important. It impacts how and if people think of you when new positions, assignments, or opportunities arise.

Your work profile should be a part of who you are authentically. Many people make the mistake of thinking that they should have one profile at work and another profile for home or other parts of their life. As I point out in *Expect to Win*, your authenticity is part of your competitive advantage. It will be difficult to do a good job while trying to maintain a work profile that is inconsistent with who you really are. You should know yourself well enough to understand the kinds of environments that will be conducive to your profile and that will allow you to thrive, and pursue an environment and a job that will value that and the contributions you can make to the organization.

Based on my experience, I've narrowed the profiles down to five categories: the good soldier, yes man, arguer, safe pair of hands, and the chief. Your profile will impact your level of responsibility, how hard you work, how assertive you have to be, how and when you are promoted, and how you are rewarded. For example, someone who is viewed as a "good soldier," who the organization feels must be retained, will generally enjoy a higher level of compensation than someone who has an "arguer," "safe pair of hands," or "yes man" profile. This is particularly true in an environment where the head of the organization is a strong leader and values people who are or who aspire to be leaders. Alternatively, someone with an arguer profile would not necessarily be as valued in an environment where the head of the organization is not a strong leader, is insecure, and has a "my way or the highway" style. Every environment has all kinds of profiles in its ecosystem and they each play a role.

The economic environment that exists when you join an organization is extremely important because the profiles that are valued and rewarded in an organization differ in various economic climates. For example, in tough economic environments, most organizations are looking for people who have the ability to get things done but also show a level of flexibility. Organizations will value someone who can execute with few resources, is constructive, complains very little, and doesn't focus on what's wrong. In a tough economic environment, you will be valued if you can show a level of creativity in getting your job done. You need a "can do" attitude. You absolutely cannot have a "Dr. No" profile—a demeanor that always points out why something *can't* be done versus showing how it *might* be done.

On the other hand, if the economic environment is strong, then you can have almost any profile. Senior managers are more tolerant of different kinds of profiles in the workplace in good times. When things are going well and there are not any resource constraints, companies look for new ideas, are willing to try new processes, and spend resources to research and develop new products. If you have an "arguer," "yes man," or "safe pair of hands" profile, your boss is likely to tolerate you because he or she might be interested in soliciting as many opinions as possible when things are going well.

When you join an organization, it is important to understand who you are, what your profile is, and how it is consistent with the organization's culture and your boss. You can also decide how you might want to further develop, improve, or change your profile. In understanding how to characterize your profile, you may want to ask yourself the following questions:

- Are you willing to make a few personal sacrifices along the way?
- Are you willing to take personal risks in your career?
- Are you willing to take on enormous responsibility?
- Are you comfortable directing or managing others?
- Are you willing to invest in the relationships that will be important to your ascending to a position of authority? Or heavily engage in what some might call corporate politics?
- Are you able to deal with setbacks in a constructive manner?
- Are you capable of managing other people or comfortable with delegating that authority to others that you might designate?
- Do you prefer that your tasks are directed by someone else or do you have the vision to take a concept and turn it into discrete tasks to execute a project?

- Are you comfortable challenging authority?
- Do you find that you are always seeking to play devil's advocate or to argue when someone offers a suggestion?

The "Good Soldier"

The "good soldier" is someone who follows orders and always executes their work correctly and in a timely fashion. He or she gets along very well with those in authority, their subordinates, and is generally well regarded by their peers. He or she follows company rules to the letter and while they may ask questions, they will rarely ever challenge the system.

The good soldier has great organizational skills and strong time management abilities. He or she may be called upon to go above and beyond their job responsibilities, and always complies and executes. They always get to work and meetings on time, rarely take sick or personal days, and manage their team or projects in an organized, systematic manner.

While this person might offer suggestions on ways to improve things or ask questions of management, he or she will never challenge those in authority. The good soldier will follow orders rather than try to find alternative ways of doing things without permission. In both good and bad economic cycles, the good soldier is generally paid within the highest quartile, but not typically at the highest level. While the good solider does an outstanding job at whatever they are told to do, they are not perceived as a superstar who contributes above and beyond others. If you are comfortable taking some personal risk, but you are most comfortable executing on others' vision rather than creating and executing on your own, then you probably fit this profile. Look for an environment where execution skills and loyalty are highly valued. Your professional growth will be strong in militaristic, hierarchal, bureaucratic environments where titles and reporting lines really matter.

Good soldiers are the perfect profile for tough economic environments, during which times organizations generally don't invest for growth, but rather seek employees who can and will continue to execute with fewer resources and little economic, technological, or human investment. They even tend to earn a premium in tough economic times. After the organization has made tough decisions, like laying off employees, the good soldier remains to execute on those decisions as prescribed by senior leadership.

When the leader of a department or organization is a good soldier, those fitting the profile are highly valued. This profile is also highly valued in an authoritative environment where the leader does not like to be challenged or has a "my way or the highway" management style. The good soldier profile does not typically thrive in highly dynamic, innovative, creative, or fast-paced environments where the prototype of success is always to question, debate, and challenge others' ideas.

The "Yes Man"

The "yes man" is someone who always agrees with those in authority, no matter what the circumstances. Unlike the good soldier, who will ask a question when something seems incorrect (but in the end will generally execute orders as given), the yes man will never openly question those in authority. The yes man believes that agreeing with the boss in all situations is the sure way to success.

In a tough economic environment, where a company is being restructured from the top down with little to no input from other team members, the yes man profile will be valued and rewarded. A yes man is also the most highly valued person in an organization when there is a tyrannical, insecure leader, with an authoritative, dictatorial management style. These leaders generally surround themselves with people who will agree with them and therefore this individual is likely to ascend to a senior position in the organization and be handsomely compensated. However, if the person you have been saying "yes" to as you have moved throughout the organization leaves the company, you will become very vulnerable to being displaced.

In a democratic organizational environment, led by a strong, secure leader, the yes man will not do well. Leaders in this environment value original thought and individual input from their team, but the yes man is not willing to risk their position by asserting an idea that is not consistent with others (and is therefore not valuable to a leader looking for that type of contribution from his or her staff).

If you are not comfortable taking personal risk or you have a "go along to get along" demeanor, then you likely identify with this profile and should look for an environment where one's ability to blindly follow orders and execute is valued.

This profile is a very low risk, safe posture to have. You can move through the junior and midlevel management ranks in almost any environment with it, but your professional growth will be a function of what is dictated to you. Trying to ascend to more senior positions will be a challenge, as most organizations will be looking to you for original thought, independent decision making, and decisiveness. You are not likely to move as far ahead as a good soldier, who has some level of personal ambition and assertiveness, or a chief, who will design and forge his or her own path.

The "Arguer"

The "arguer" is someone who always has a devil's advocate approach. They are the person who challenges any idea that is introduced. People with this profile identify the negative side of the "what if" scenario and are very difficult to get on board with new ideas, especially those that are revolutionary or new to the company. They are generally not fans of any ideas that require new thinking, new behavior, or the adoption of new processes and procedures.

In a highly innovative environment, like at a technology company, this profile will be valued. These kinds of organizations need someone who is vocal and always pushing the limits on new ideas. They demand employees who can anticipate the downside scenarios so that the company can respond and proceed to market with the idea.

The arguer will thrive in an environment where the leader is extremely secure, accomplished in his or her own right, and has a long track record of success, particularly as an innovator. If the leader has worked in a start-up environment, either within a large corporation or a small company, and he or she has had a history of failure, the big WIN, failure, and then the big WIN again, then they will be comfortable being challenged by this person. In fact, they will welcome it. They will value the arguer type because they view that demeanor as a catalyst for the management or execution team to arrive at the best outcomes. In this type of leadership environment, this profile will be invited onto the senior management team, be well compensated, and will generally be given opportunities to manage teams responsible for producing new products.

In environments where the leader is a "my way or the highway" type and does not like to be challenged, the arguer will not fare well and is likely to be ignored, not well compensated, or even fired. The only way that an arguer will survive in this kind of environment is if he or she has a special skill or talent that is needed by the organization and is difficult to find.

The "Safe Pair of Hands"

The "safe pair of hands" is a younger version of the "good soldier" profile and is usually found among junior and midlevel people in the organization. Like the good soldier, the safe pair of hands generally won't challenge authority and executes tasks with little to no pushback regarding process or rationale. They are meticulous about their work, are focused on execution almost to a fault, and are perceived as someone who can be trusted to get the job done correctly and in a timely manner. The Safe Pair of Hands will not assert themselves, but rather are passive in the environment and squarely focused on executing on whatever tasks they are given. They are generally not innovators and will not expend personal capital or take the risk to offer up new ideas in the environment.

If you have this profile, senior people will want to work with you. You will be requested for team assignments and your ability to execute will be highly valued. However, when it is time to think of people to be promoted, you won't be among the first to be elevated if you haven't had a chance to show people that (in addition to your execution skills) you are also a strategic problem solver. The safe pair of hands does well in both good and bad economic environments, but thrives most in an autocratic or militaristic environment where leaders place a high value on execution capabilities, and will compensate this profile handsomely. In an economically challenging environment where there is a lot of restructuring to implement and execute, the safe pair of hands will flourish. This profile will also succeed in a fast-paced, innovative environment where there is a clear division of labor between those that innovate and those that implement to get the product to market.

The "Chief"

The "chief" is someone who has strong vision, strong management skills, outstanding execution, and is perceived to have the ability to motivate others and drive the organization forward in any economic environment. This person has a healthy appetite for taking risks in the organization. They are always the person who will step up to lead a new business, try a new process, or go after a tough client. The chief is likely to thrive no matter the current economy. In a tough economic environment, they won't be afraid to make the tough decisions or to live by them. And in good economic environments, they will be willing to be aggressive in pursuing opportunities.

The chief is unafraid to challenge the leadership's point of view and question assignments, and is also usually the person who is recognized to have the strongest performance or the most influential voice in the organization. The chief is comfortable taking personal risk to contribute an innovative idea in meetings or challenging others' ideas or execution. This profile will thrive in an environment with a secure leader who values being challenged, and having team members who are assertive and have an appetite for risk. In an insecure leadership environment, the chief profile will not be valued or rewarded because the leader does not like to be challenged.

No Matter Your Profile, You Can
Become a Leader

As I said at the outset of this chapter, all types of profiles exist in a work environment. Whether a profile survives or thrives depends on the type of economic and leadership environment that exists in the organization. No matter what your profile is, however, it is important to know that you can still be a great leader in your organization. Before we end this chapter, I would like to offer you a few thoughts on what I believe are the key attributes of a good leader, but first let's talk about what you have to do to transition your profile to be able to lead.

If you are a good soldier, you already have strong execution skills, a track record of achievement in your organization, and a solid reputation. In order to transition to a position of leadership, you have to demonstrate that you have vision and can articulate ideas effectively to teams of people. You also have to demonstrate that you are comfortable not only challenging authority, but moving forward when it is clear that the leadership is not 100 percent on board.

If you are the yes man profile, you will have to show your organization that you are willing to articulate a dissenting opinion to whatever thoughts your leadership has articulated. You will not only have to exhibit this behavior once but many times, in order for the organization to believe that you will stand up for what you believe in as opposed to going along with the popular or mandated directive. If those that are to follow you do not believe that you will stand up for what you believe is right, they are not likely to follow you as a leader.

If you are the argumentative type, then you have to become more collaborative in order to be able to lead people and to encourage them to offer their best ideas to you as a leader. If people think that you will always offer the opposing point of view and will challenge them on every idea that they offer up, they will simply stop taking the risks to offer innovative or unpopular ideas. Pretty soon, you will have a team of people working with you that will only execute orders and never offer innovative ideas, which will compromise your success as a leader.

If you have the chief profile, you already have the basic characteristics to be a great leader. Your comfort with challenging authority, new ideas, and contribution from others will inspire other people to work with you. You have an appetite for risk that is a hallmark for impactful leadership and your execution skills and track record will enable you to solicit and garner the respect from those around you.

When I think of the profile of a powerful, impactful, authentic leader, I think of characteristics that revolve around the letters in the word l-e-a-d-e-r.

L Is for Leverage

Great leaders understand the concept of *leverage*. They know that there is no monopoly on intellect. They will not always be the one with the best idea, the best answer, or the best strategy. Therefore, they understand how important it is to leverage the ideas and thoughts of others.

Great leaders know how to inspire and harness the best abilities of those around them, and know how to use their team's ideas about new products, processes, and customers to inform or develop the best product, outcome, or execution for their team, project, or company. Leaders strive to create an environment where their team members feel encouraged to assert and share their ideas and thoughts. A great leader will convince others that they should be invested in the team's success and will motivate them to contribute.

A great leader creates an atmosphere where people are motivated to contribute creative, out-of-the-box, risky ideas, and are not afraid to fail. When one person contributes an idea that is accepted, the leader acknowledges the person, but also makes sure to reward the team for the outcome. A strong leader is a heavy user of the "we" pronoun over the "I" or the "you."

A good leader also understands that he or she should be a point of leverage for his or her boss or senior management as well. No matter where you are in your career, there is always someone ahead of you. If you are a vice president, there is an executive vice president or senior vice president that you report to. If you are a president, there is a CEO that you answer to. Even the CEO has to report to the chairman of the board. Whether or not you like him or her is irrelevant. Part of delivering your assignment or executing your role with excellence is outperforming your superior's expectations so you can maximize your success, and if you so desire, continue to ascend to the top.

If you want to be a great leader, you should use the ideas that your team contributes as the basis for the execution of the project or product. This is what it means to leverage the talent of your team. You do not have to be responsible for creating or developing the answer; instead you use the intellect of your team, their creativity, and their contributions.

E Is for Efficiency

Great leaders are *efficient in communicating*. They create clear processes, strategies, and directions that their team understands, and they are transparent about the outcome they are seeking. Leaders create a common understanding among the team of what success looks like, so that each individual is clear on what role they play and what it takes for them to achieve outstanding performance.

A great leader will define what success looks like for the team. What revenue outcome is the team trying to achieve? What deadline is important to meet? How much cost do they want to eliminate from the budget? How many new customers do they want to attract? What is the rate of customer adoption that they aspire to? A good leader knows that if their team is not clear on what success looks like individually and collectively, the team will not perform well and each individual on the team will not contribute all that they have to offer to the team. The worst-case scenario outcome will be that the leader will get subpar performance from the team. The best-case scenario is that they'll get a result that might be acceptable, but it is not optimal and does not maximize the team's productivity or achieve the leader's goals and objectives.

A great leader goes out of his or her way to make sure that the team stays focused, committed, and motivated to produce excellence every day. They make sure to create an environment where their team is not distracted by internal politics or other exogenous factors, such as the broader economy, unemployment rates, and so on.

These leaders make it easy for their team members to focus on doing their job well. They make sure their team is not working in a vacuum, hoping for an outcome that the boss deems good. Instead, they have a very clear list of goals, time lines, and expectations. The team is always aware of where they are in relation to their goals.

Another component of being an efficient leader is providing timely feedback to your team, both good and bad. One of the advantages of being an efficient leader is that it makes it easier to offer negative feedback to a team member who is not performing up to your expectations, because you have clearly defined your expectations of each team member. As we discussed in Chapter 6, many organizations do not give clear feedback, and it is therefore difficult to counsel someone out of your company and off of your team when you haven't given clear feedback about their poor performance. If, however, you have clearly defined what success looks like and your expectations for their performance, it is a clear cut and easy conversation to have if they do not deliver consistent with what you have outlined. When you provide a clear road map to success, and when a team member for whatever reason does not measure up, you can clearly articulate why you are changing their assignment, demoting them, or in some cases replacing them.

While it is never easy to provide negative feedback to someone, it is perceived to be a much fairer process when the expectations were clearly provided at the outset. Alternatively, when you want to reward someone for an exceptional job, it is also easy to point out to others why someone has exceeded the goals—again, because the goals were clearly laid out from the beginning.

If you cannot articulate your expectations at the outset of a project, or when a new member joins your team, you are not a very strong leader. Being a leader requires having a detailed vision of what success for your team, your department, and your company looks like. Your job as a leader is to clearly articulate the definition of success and to offer ways in which individuals might execute on that success.

A Is for Action

A great leader knows when it is time to *act*. You cannot inspire people to follow you if they think that when it is time to make a decision or to move a plan forward that you will hesitate. Demonstrating this willingness also encourages the people around you to apply that same timing to their work as well.

I once heard Meg Whitman, former CEO of eBay and current CEO of Hewlett Packard, speak at a conference. She said, "The price of inaction is greater than the cost of making a mistake." That is one of the most profound and important statements I have ever heard about acting as a leader. The quote stuck with me because it underscores the notion that there is a price to be paid for not acting, particularly in critical business situations. A great leader is decisive in their actions. They know that in a crisis, time is generally not a friend, and that swift and thoughtful decisions lead to strong actions that result in a definitive outcome, good or bad.

Being seen as a decisive person will encourage others to think their ideas through and present them to you along with a plan for execution and implementation, knowing that because it won't take you long to make a yes/no call, they must be ready to move the idea forward.

This is an exciting environment for highly motivated, talented individuals to work in. They will want to work for and with you, share their ideas, and risk offering out-of-the-box ideas that could make your organization more efficient, more productive, and/or enhance profitability.

Sometimes we don't want to act because we are afraid of making a mistake. But as I wrote in *Expect to Win*, and as I continue to say in my speeches, "FEAR has no place in your success equation; anytime that you operate from a position of fear, you will ALWAYS underpenetrate any opportunity."

If you have studied a situation and solicited ideas from your people and other colleagues, then act on the best choice that you can make at that time.

D Is for Diversity

A great leader also understands that there is no monopoly on intelligence and that in order to get the best ideas, they must make sure that there is a diverse group of people around the table who are involved in coming up with solutions, solving problems, or making decisions.

These days, when people talk about *diversity* and inclusion, they are often squarely focused on the idea that "it is the right thing," ethically, morally, socially, and politically, to have racial, gender, or ethnic diversity at the decision-making table. While I agree with this, I'd like to offer another perspective for positioning yourself as a champion of diversity.

No matter what industry you work in, innovation in some manner is essential for success and even survival in today's highly competitive global business environment. It is the key to obtaining and retaining leadership and a competitive sustainable advantage. To be innovative, whether it's regarding product format, packaging, size, price, functionality, or speed, you need to have people who are comfortable with taking risks and thinking of a solution from every possible perspective.

Diverse ideas are a necessity to give birth to innovative ideas and solutions. In order to get diverse ideas, you need diverse perspectives, and in order to get diverse perspectives, you need diverse experiences. Finally, in order to get diverse experiences, you need people from diverse backgrounds—those who have experienced the world differently and therefore look at problems and develop innovative ideas by looking through different lenses. Having a diverse workplace is not just the right thing to do—it's essential for success.

E Is for Engaged

A great leader knows how to truly *engage* the people who work for them. They engage them in conversations, not only about work, but also about themselves, their families, and their hobbies. They try to know them as people, not just as the professional who delivers a work product every day. As a leader, the more you engage the people that work for you, the more connected they will feel not only to you, but to the team, the project, and even the company.

Engaging people is also about offering them liberal praise for a job well done. When the people on your team do a great job, even a good job, you should let them know directly and sometimes publicly, in front of other team members or members of a department. When you show that you appreciate the efforts people make, they are likely to expend even more effort on the next task or project. It is human nature to respond positively when someone regularly applauds your hard work. We all enjoy getting good feedback. In fact, we feel more confident about our ability to consistently deliver results if our work is regularly affirmed by the person who evaluates us. Or perhaps something has gone wrong. If you have connected with the people who work for you, it is much easier to deliver a poor performance report or review, or to admonish the team who hasn't delivered. The trust you've built will serve to ensure that critical feedback will be seen as constructive and those at fault are more likely to move quickly to correct a problem and be mindful not to repeat it in the future.

To be a great leader, it's also important to understand what it takes to motivate each person on your team. Everyone is different. Some people are motivated by money, while for others it is a title, and for still others it could be simple, consistent recognition or challenging assignments. If you want the best from each of your direct reports, your job is to discover what motivates each of them, and then engage them by offering them the specific motivation they need to consistently deliver excellence.

R Is for Responsible and Responsive

A great leader feels and acts *responsible* for their team, its actions and results, and truly owns the outcomes of the group's endeavors, good or bad. "It happened on my watch, so I own it" is the attitude of a great leader. They take the blame when their team messes up, and rarely try to shift it to someone else. This is not to say that a good leader won't reprimand a team member if they don't deliver. In fact, a good leader will hold all of the team members accountable for their specific roles. But strong leaders know that it's their job to give the team members the support, direction, guidance, resources, and whatever else they need to succeed.

In addition to taking responsibility for outcomes, strong leaders are also *responsive* to their people. If a team member has an issue, a challenge, or a question that must be answered so that the team's objectives can be advanced, a good leader will make it a priority to respond immediately. Good leaders understand that if they are not responsive to their people, they will create an environment where people don't share their challenges in executing the tasks at hand and it will put the completion of the work at hand in peril. In addition, if the team anticipates that the leader will take a long time to make a decision they will not approach the work with a sense of urgency toward completion, and productivity will suffer as a result.

◀ *Carla's Pearls* ▶

1. Be self-aware. Know your profile and what it says about you. Are you the "good soldier," the "yes man," the "arguer," the "safe pair of hands," or the "chief"?
2. Your profile affects how and if people think of you when new positions, assignments, or opportunities to lead arise.
3. No matter what your profile is, you can be a leader in your environment.
4. Great leaders understand the importance of leverage, efficiency, and action; and are decisive, diversity focused, engaged, and responsible.

STARTING OVER

CHAPTER 8

Knowing When It's Time to Make a Change

"When you are through changing, you are through."
—Bruce Barton

The decision to change jobs is one of the most important decisions you'll make during your career, and one that you'll likely make several times over. In this chapter, we'll closely examine the reasons you might want to consider moving from one organization to another (for a detailed discussion on changing jobs within an organization, see my previous book, *Expect to Win*). In addition, I'll offer you a framework you might want to use when thinking about changing careers.

Before we get too far into the conversation, let's start with the assumption that after careful consideration and due diligence, you made the choice to join your current employer because it fit in with your career goals, you liked the people and culture, and were satisfied with the career trajectory the company offered. In other words, you didn't stumble into the job or take it just to have one.

If you have made the decision to join a company and you thought that it was the right one for you, under what circumstances should you ever consider leaving? There are a few reasons for a move to a new organization. You move because:

1. You are looking for significantly greater compensation.
2. You want a role with a new and different platform that offers greater responsibility, career trajectory, or power.
3. You want a different career trajectory.
4. You are not being treated fairly.
5. You have to go.

Significantly Greater Compensation

Andrew works as a middle-level manager at an industrial engineering firm. His goal is to become an officer and manage a product department that is a significant revenue contributor to his company. He has been at the firm for eight years. Based on his last evaluation, he won't be eligible for a promotion to vice president for another two years. Further, the promotion would be dependent on the company continuing to do well and the current vice president in his division moving into a more senior role or to another firm.

Because the company has not performed very well due to the economic crisis and competitive pressures, Andrew has not enjoyed a significant increase in compensation for the last two years. One day, Andrew received a call from a competitor's senior vice president inviting him to lunch. The SVP is not only familiar with Andrew's work, but also knows the specific challenges that Andrew's firm is experiencing. During their lunch, he offers Andrew an opportunity to run his firm's industrial engineering department for a new product rapidly gaining market share. He would be a vice president in this new role, where he would be evaluated based on the revenue he generates (putting him on track for a promotion to executive vice president in eighteen months and a salary increase of 100 percent along with stock options).

With this offer, Andrew has an opportunity to double his salary, accelerate his promotion by two years, and has a clear path to his next promotion. In this case, he is certainly being compensated for the risks of moving with the new opportunity platform as well as pay and other benefits. Further, he would be working for a company that is on track to becoming a market leader, while his current company is struggling to compete and is slow to change. At the new firm, he would also have the opportunity to put points on the board early in his tenure because the company is in the same industry as his current job, and he knows the business very well.

If you have an opportunity to markedly accelerate your career path and multiply your compensation, as Andrew does in this scenario, making the change from one company to another is definitely worthwhile, particularly if it's in the same industry and requires the same types of skills you use in your current job. In this case, the decision is clear.

Where the decision to change companies gets a little murky is when the prospective new company is promising you a promotion *after* you make the decision to join the company and *after* a period of time. Here, significant risk is being introduced into the equation. If a company makes you an offer with a promise for a promotion after a predetermined amount of time, you should make sure that you understand the exact parameters and conditions required for you to receive the promotion. You must also be comfortable and clear on how you will react if you don't get it and what your options are for moving forward at the company or potentially moving on.

Sally was offered a position at a high-profile retail company. Since she would be starting in her new role during the middle of the second quarter of the company's fiscal year, the recruiter told her they "did not want to upset the culture and bring someone in from the outside with the same title as the person leaving the role." Assuming she performed well, Sally was promised that the promotion was hers at the end of the year.

The prospective firm also offered Sally a starting salary equal to what she was making in her current job. She was told she would receive a salary increase along with the promised promotion at the end of the year. Sally accepted the position on the verbal promise that these things would come to pass. She performed exceedingly well in her new role and hit every goal that she and her manager had agreed upon. However, the company did not do well overall; two of the key senior leaders who helped recruit Sally left the company; and the organization lost significant market share relative to its peers.

As a result, Sally did not get her raise or promotion. She was told by human resources that not only were promotions not ever guaranteed (especially because she didn't have an agreement in writing), but that the company's bad year meant that promotions were rare at that time. Since the two executives who recruited her were no longer with the company, she had no one to hold accountable or even complain to.

What can Sally do in this situation? She essentially has two choices. First, she could have a serious conversation with human resources about how she feels the company did a bait and switch with respect to the assurances they made when she was hired. In that conversation, she could seek to get a bona fide path to promotion in the next year. Second, she could leave the company. The choice that she makes depends on how much she trusts the organization to make good on any new assurances and whether she is confident that the person she prospectively chooses as a sponsor will have the power to convince others she should have the promotion. If Sally has lost all confidence in the company's ability to honor its commitments, then seeking an opportunity at an organization where her skills and experience will be valued and rewarded is probably the right call.

Another potential situation to be aware of is when a company makes you an offer to start in a role that has never existed before. While the compensation may be handsome and the role might sound powerful, be careful to do your due diligence, making sure they are committed to this new path. Many times, companies have aspirations to change, grow, and start something new, but those aspirations are often connected to a charismatic leader and not necessarily embraced by the rest of the organization, the board of directors, or the company's officers. Sometimes making such a shift in the company's operating profile is not fully thought through, nor does it have the full commitment of leadership.

Seema was hired as the new director of sales for a medical device company. Until her hire, the company had a decentralized sales and marketing process. Individual territory managers had their own sales and marketing professionals, and each was responsible for developing and implementing the sales strategy for the company's product in their respective markets. The company felt it would be more efficient and create greater scale and brand consistency to have a centralized sales and marketing function for all the geographical locations in a territory. When Seema started, she hired a couple of new people, but for the most part she worked with the people already deployed in the field.

She created a new strategy and operating instructions, but many of the salespeople continued to adhere to the old localized approach, and so Seema's plan failed miserably. After one year, the company abandoned the centralized approach, reassigned Seema, and reverted to the old way of doing things. While the company thought it wanted to change, it didn't put a structure in place that would support Seema and the new methodology. Further, they didn't stick with the new direction long enough to assess whether it was better than the old one. While Seema was not fired, neither she nor her new methodology were ever fully embraced, which will make it hard for her to recover from this failure. Seema should seek to move on to another opportunity outside the firm.

When you are being hired as a change agent, you should make sure that you have a clear understanding of how committed the company is to the new methodology, as well as of its history of success (or failure) to make revolutionary changes. You should ask questions like:

- What is the time line for implementing the change?
- How long will we have to evaluate the new change?
- What incentives can we use to motivate the team to quickly embrace the change?
- What abilities do I have to make changes to the current team?
- How will we measure success?
- Has the company ever tried to change its methodology or process? How long ago? Was it a success or failure? How long did it take to adopt the new change?

If you believe your potential employer is really committed to following through on making a change, then there are a few things that you must do in order to make sure that you are successful in developing and/or implementing the change.

First you must be able to articulate the new strategy clearly. This includes the "why": why the change is an improvement over the old way things are being done; the "what": what will be different from the old process; the "how": how will the new change be implemented; and the "who": who will be affected and who will be responsible for making it happen. The people that you are introducing the change to will naturally be concerned or question the potential success of the new process. No one wants to be a part of something that might not work. The clearer you are about these factors, the easier it will be for people to start believing that the new process has a chance to succeed and get on board.

Second, you need to establish credibility that you know how to do the job and implement the new strategy. When you are new to an organization, one way to do this is to have your boss introduce you to the organization, specifically citing what you were brought in to do and your credentials to do so. Then it's up to you to demonstrate that you have a core competency with the new process or that you have the ability to coordinate and execute a vision.

Third, you must make a good assessment of your team. You want to ask such questions as, Who are the thought leaders? Who are the skeptics? Who are the "say no to everything" people? Who are the loyalists to the old regime? Who are likely to be the early adopters? Who has the capability and skill to perform well with the new way of doing things? Who does not have the ability or the desire to make the change? Understanding the players on your team will be important to your ability to be successful in implementing change. Identifying the early adopters as soon as possible will help you convert the other team members. In fact, you want them to help you "infect" the other members in the organization with the enthusiasm and optimism about the success of the new process. One way to do this is to have a few respected members of the team work directly with you on a task so they can get to know you, your capabilities, and your intellect firsthand. Be collaborative and team oriented while also articulating your expertise. Your team members will tell others in the organization about their experience with you.

It is crucial to understand who is the most resistant; who is actively working against the change; or even who is working against it by simply not executing as instructed, by articulating skepticism, or by making negative comments to other team members about the success of the new process. You must move quickly to convert those who are creating doubt, or have them reassigned to another project, team, or department. When you first take on the assignment, you want to make sure that you have the ability to make staffing changes to your new team. You cannot afford to have one or two people cause your plan to fail, particularly after you have established your credibility and clearly articulated a vision and plan of execution.

If you find that you need to make changes to the team, you should do so quickly. When you are slow about doing such things, it's easy to exacerbate natural feelings of uneasiness among remaining team members, which then can grow into a general feeling of insecurity and then, even worse, productivity paralysis. If people are not sure that they will continue to have a place in the organization, then they start to worry, the negative water cooler chatter intensifies, and then the productivity level of the organization decreases, and professionals potentially start to get distracted with looking outside of the organization for other jobs. If you quickly change members of the team, then you can announce to the organization that the changes are complete and that the team is moving forward with the new plan.

Last, you must establish clear metrics around the changes being implemented and celebrate the accomplishments of milestones. Set up a few easy wins for the organization or team. Ideally, there will be clear milestones that the team needs to accomplish on the way to full execution. As the team reaches the milestones, more optimism will be created around the possibility and probability of success of the change. More and more, the organization will embrace and adopt the change, as evidence is created about the effectiveness of the plan. You will realize your success as a change agent!

New and Different Platform That Offers Greater Career Trajectory or Power

Eileen was a senior marketing executive at a major consumer products company. She had direct profit and loss level responsibility and was on the senior marketing steering committee. Eileen had a voice at the table regarding the direction of marketing protocol and strategy that impacted many of her firm's brands. Eileen received a call from an executive search firm with a financial services firm client that had determined that it was in a war for talent and that they needed a brand management approach to recruiting and retaining top employees. The client was looking for someone to set global human resources and communications strategy and develop a new, innovative approach to talent management, positioning the company as an employer of choice in the highly competitive talent market.

The recruiter told Eileen that the company was willing to consider hiring people from outside the human resources and financial services arenas and would pay three times her current salary. She would also be offered a global role on the company's operating and management committee, giving her international exposure that she did not currently have. She would be reporting directly to the CEO with quarterly exposure to the company's board of directors and oversight of the company's twenty thousand employees. Eileen thought that it was a compelling opportunity with the chance to impact the company's future. She interviewed with the company's current senior team and members of the management committee, and had an informal meeting with two members of the board of directors, after which the company made her an offer. Eileen knew if she accepted the position she would be taking a significant risk. In her current role, she had power and influence. Even though it was at the department and not the company level, she had a management committee position. Eileen also had significant performance currency at her current firm and a reputation as one of the best brand managers in the industry. She fit into her company's culture, understood the politics, and could see a clear trajectory to the top marketing role within just a couple of years.

Should she accept the new position, Eileen knew she would take on the risk of working in a completely new industry, financial services, with its reputation for being highly competitive, regulated, dynamic, and intense. Choosing a person who did not have a financial services track record was bound to be greeted with skepticism by many members of the organization. Plus, the company was embarking on a completely new direction to talent management, which could meet with resistance. As she considered the substantial risks, Eileen also thought about the level at which she would be compensated for those risks. She had "air cover"—direct access to the CEO. This was his directive and he was going to sell it to the company and to the board. She would also have direct contact with the board at least once a quarter and could also directly market herself and her ideas, and build her own relationships with them. In addition to getting equity in the company, her salary would increase significantly; she'd have global exposure and greater opportunity; and a stellar team of people—the entire organization—at her disposal.

In the end, the opportunities outweighed the risks and

Eileen would be highly compensated for those risks. She took the job, changing firms and roles.

Different Career Trajectory

There may be a time when it makes sense to leave a company because you want to focus on a completely different career. For example, you work in a for-profit, corporate environment and you want to pursue a leadership job in a nonprofit organization. Or you work in corporate training and would like to pursue a job in academics, perhaps teaching at a university.

In each case, it makes perfect sense to make a change. Most of us will work for thirty years or more, and you should work in an organization and in a career that will make you happy and will fulfill those objectives that you want to accomplish. And chances are, your objectives might change over the course of a long working life.

If you are going to leave one career for another, make sure that you have gone through the exercises that we talk about in Chapter 1—the Content Page, the Jobs Page, the Skills, Experience, Education Page—and that you have updated your career agenda. Have prepared a full assessment of your strengths, weaknesses, and experiences so that you can leverage them when you are interviewing for a position in the new industry. You must also be able to answer these questions: Why this industry? Why now? Why didn't you pursue it before now? Why do you think it's a good time to make the career switch?

When you are making a career or industry change, your network will be one of the most important tools in your tool chest. When you are in college or graduate school, employers will come to you as they visit your campus to hire new recruits, but once you have graduated, the best way to make a change successfully is to access the relationships in your network. You should start to talk to various people about your desire to change industries and try to leverage each conversation for information that you might need to be successful in the new role or an introduction to a person who might lead you to the new opportunity.

There are various sites where you can simply e-mail a résumé in an attempt to get a new opportunity, but most often the people who are sorting through those résumés are specifically looking for someone who has the prerequisite or similar industry experience to fill the role. As a result, if you are switching careers, there is a high probability that your résumé will be ignored. The most effective way to make your case about switching careers is to get an opportunity to be face-to-face with the decision maker, and your network can introduce you to that person.

Alternatively, perhaps you are ready to breathe life into your entrepreneurial ideas and start your own company. If you are thinking about starting something on your own, please make sure that you do not leave your current position until you have the capital necessary to start your business and see it through its first year of operation. Or, at the very least, have a concrete plan around how you will raise the needed capital and a solid plan for operational execution. It is important that you have thought through how you are going to market, promote, and sell your product or service, at what price, and through what distribution channel. You should think about who you will have work with you and what your exit strategies are for the business. Are you trying to grow the business large enough to take the company public, have an initial public market (IPO) exit? Or are you trying to grow and develop the business so that it will be attractive to a buyer, a larger competitor and have an M&A exit? I could go on and on about how to make a successful transition from working for someone to starting your own business, but that will have to be in another book, as it is too detailed to cover here.

Not Being Treated Fairly

In my experience, most companies generally have good human resources policies. They may even have strong, well-intentioned directives from the top of the organization. But often that demeanor of fairness and equitable treatment does not trickle down to the rest of the organization. As they say, "all politics is local." And so it is within the corporate environment. The leadership of an organization is responsible for defining the culture, exhibiting the cultural dynamics, and holding other leaders and managers accountable. Then it is the individual managers, department, and division heads who are responsible for implementing the culture.

This is where the culture of fairness lives and dies. If an individual manager does not treat the people in his or her department fairly, then over time, good people will leave. Unfortunately, it may be a long time before the company's leadership in a large organization notices that a particular department is losing good people, and an even longer time before the problem can be traced back to an individual manager. This is especially true if the company does not have accountability in the review process, or a practice of conducting exit interviews and not properly reviewing the feedback (or not doing exit interviews at all).

Even when companies have built-in mechanisms to allow employees to report unfair treatment, doing so takes courage.

Professionals are often afraid of the possible repercussions. So rather than coming forward with an issue, most simply decide to move on to other opportunities, leaving the company in the dark about why it is losing good people.

If you find yourself in a situation where you think you are a victim of unfair treatment, the first thing to do is raise the issue with a senior person, preferably the person who is your boss, even if you think that the boss is the person who is not treating you fairly. Approach the conversation seeking to gain a better understanding of the circumstances. It is possible that what you perceive as a slight may be the result of something you did or perhaps failed to do. I am a big believer in checking yourself first. Your goal in this conversation is to confirm that this person is or is not treating you unfairly. In many cases, the clearest example of inequitable treatment is demonstrated when you don't get a promotion that you believe you deserve, or you believe that you are paid less than other people who are performing in a comparable role in a comparable way, or you are not getting the same type of assignments or clients that other people are receiving.

Let's assume for example that you feel that you have been mistreated because you did not get promoted at the same time as some of your peers. The ensuing conversation with your manager, human resources liaison, or another decision maker regarding your promotion should go something like this:

"Robert, I wanted to check in with you to see if I am reading this situation correctly. My performance is at a level expected for someone with my skills and experience. I have consistently received good reviews. In the last few promotion cycles however, I have not been considered for promotion and I am not sure why. Is there something I am missing in my portfolio of skills that makes me ineligible? How can I raise this issue in a constructive manner to get consideration the next time around or at least to gain an understanding of what I need to do to make myself an attractive and eligible promotion candidate?"

This approach is nonconfrontational and will open the door for a frank conversation that will likely elicit a response that offers you constructive feedback or insight. At the same time, it gives you an opportunity to further iterate your interest in getting promoted.

On the other hand, if you approach the conversation in a confrontational manner, it is highly unlikely you will receive an open, useful response. Instead, your manager is likely to be defensive and measured and careful in his reply in an attempt to calm and contain the conversation. Remember, you have two primary goals in this discussion: to communicate your desire for a promotion and to find out why you have not been promoted.

Depending on what your manager says, a secondary, more subtle goal is to communicate that you feel you may have been treated unfairly. If the feedback you receive is constructive and there doesn't appear to be a strong reason for the lack of promotion, then I would suggest you continue the conversation like this:

"Robert, based on your feedback, it seems like I have met all of the criteria for being promoted, yet it has not happened. I feel like I have been treated unfairly and am not sure why that is the case. What can we do together to rectify the situation?"

You should also be prepared to speak to your boss's boss in an effort to get another perspective and to also make someone else in your organization aware, someone who could potentially change or impact the situation.

This approach to the discussion will put you on the path toward rectifying matters. Or, at the very least, launch a series of conversations and events that will further clarify for you where you stand in the organization and its commitment (or lack thereof) to you as a professional. If after several conversations and an appropriate amount of time (within twelve months), there is no significant change in your professional status, then perhaps it is time to make a change.

You Have to Go!

There may be times in your career when you can clearly see the handwriting on the wall: the company announces it is shutting down the product line where you work; it has plans to lay off 10 percent of its workforce, and you know that your last few performance reviews have not been good; you recently made a major career-limiting mistake and your boss has told you it is a good time to consider opportunities outside the firm; you've learned that the company plans a restructuring and you are likely to be affected. If any of these scenarios sounds familiar, then you are reading the situation clearly, it is time to make a change . . . you have to go!

Before you do so, however, make sure you have exhausted all opportunities at your current firm. Just because a company is getting out of a particular product line doesn't mean it can't use your expertise elsewhere. A planned layoff situation doesn't necessarily mean you will be among those let go. You may have some skill or attribute the company plans to deploy in another department. Or perhaps you have relationships at the company where someone is willing to use his or her capital on your behalf to save you even if your job is eliminated. When you find yourself in a situation like this, your network of relationships—especially your relationship with your mentor or sponsor—will be particularly useful.

Your sponsor can offer insight into what is really going on

at the company, and in what capacity, if any, he or she will work to keep you at the company if you desire to stay. If it turns out your job is likely to be eliminated and your sponsor can't do anything to change that, then you can solicit his or her advice about other opportunities or about the best way to leave the company without burning bridges. You always want to leave a company with a potential opportunity to return. Strategies, leadership, and decision makers change, and you never know when you might want to come back.

Once you have determined it is time to leave, start looking for opportunities. Whenever possible, you don't want to wait until someone says you have to go, especially if you are not leaving because of circumstances beyond your control (e.g., the company is changing or eliminating a product line).

The Risks in Making a Change

Anytime you leave one organization and join another, there are risks involved, including the following:

- The new role is not as important as you were told.
- The person who sponsored you into the organization leaves before you have an opportunity to build your own network of supporters.
- The company changes its strategy before or shortly after you start.
- The leadership and direction of the company, and/or that of your department, changes shortly after you arrive.
- You don't have access to all of the resources you were promised.

- The key players on the team you planned to work with quit before you have a real opportunity to establish yourself as the new leader, and now you are faced with the prospect of hiring a new team, delaying your ability to deliver on what you promised when you were recruited.

And then one of the biggest risks: that you did not do proper due diligence when you were considering the company and it turns out you made a real mistake and this is not the organization for you—its values, direction, and culture are the antithesis to what you value as a professional.

It is highly possible that any one of the preceding could happen when you move from one organization to another. Even if everything appears to be as you envision it, there are still risks when you move to a new role. As a new person in the environment, you have to put points on the board quickly in order to communicate to the rest of the professionals and to the person who hired you that you were a good choice, and there is always a risk that you might not be able to execute as fast as you should.

You must consider the other players (the sponsors, the supporters, the "say no to everything" people, and the saboteurs); the economic dynamics (a good vs. bad economic environment); and the availability of resources and other considerations that could be characterized as risks (technology, product, or operational). You should also make sure that you are compensated for these risks.

When making job or career moves, most people are so consumed with the details of making the change that they forget to evaluate whether they are being compensated properly for the chance they are taking by changing jobs. It is rarely, if ever, advisable to change organizations for exactly the same amount of compensation. Yes, there may be extenuating circumstances or family pressures that sometimes make this necessary. But realize that when you move for the exact same level of compensation, you are essentially taking on a role for less money. As we discussed previously, there are risks and potential costs associated with being the newest person in a different company that did not exist in your old role at your previous company.

Even if you are unhappy in your current environment and really want out, don't allow emotion to drive you to a new job for the same compensation. You can and should argue for more pay and benefits to compensate you for the risks associated with making a move, being the newest employee, and the deliverables you are now responsible for. You can also argue for greater pay because of the applicable skills and experience that you are bringing to the new role. Don't allow yourself to be held hostage by your current salary. Think about it. Why would you leave an organization where people know you and where you know the good, the bad, and the ugly about the company and how to navigate the culture and politics of the organization, for an unknown situation paying exactly the same salary?

To avoid that scenario, here is a sample of how you might broach this with a prospective employer (this could be your potential boss or the HR representative):

"While I am currently making X, I understand the market salary for my position is Y. I have the skills and experience to deliver at the highest level that the role demands and I am seeking/expecting compensation consistent with that performance."

Remember, it's not about the salary you are currently making. It is about the incentive for you to move!

There is one scenario that might justify changing jobs for the same salary and that is if you are moving from one industry to another. While you are taking on more risks as the new person in the organization, the new employer is also taking a risk with you because you have no previous history in this new industry. One could reason that a lower relative salary (meaning the same salary plus the risks that you are not being compensated for) is justified because of the investment that you are making in yourself to learn a new industry and the risk that the company is taking on you.

When you start working in a new organization, there are a number of things you will have to do. You will have to:

- reestablish your performance currency
- find a sponsor in the organization
- learn the rules of the game associated with this new environment
- identify and categorize the players in the organization

Framework for Changing Jobs and/or Careers

Given the rapid pace at which technology is disrupting traditional businesses and industries, and the swift creation of new industries, companies, and functions, if you're a Millennial, it's likely that you'll have three to four careers within the span of a thirty- or forty-year working life.

Many jobs filling the landscape today did not exist a decade ago. Consider Facebook. The company was just getting started in 2004, and Twitter and Instagram did not even exist. The entire social media industry was simply an idea a short time ago and now it is at the center of our existence as human beings. The content of traditional roles like chief operating officer and chief information officer have also changed dramatically. Titles like head of human capital management, chief franchise officer, and chief of cyber-security did not exist at the turn of this century and are now integral positions in some of the largest multibillion-dollar public companies in the world. Given this dynamic, how do you know when it is time for you to change careers?

If you are thinking of changing careers, the first step is to consider your personal career agenda, as we discussed in Chapters 1 and 2. Your career agenda analyzes what skills, experiences, and intellectual content you want to acquire over the course of your career; your goals around compensation, title, authority, and power; and a time line for accomplishing your goals.

Let's call the particular job you are focused on "the seat." You should also have a personal agenda ancillary to your professional goals that considers family, relationships, community, philanthropy, spirituality, and whatever else is important to you outside of work. Finally, you should have a reason why you want to work at a particular company. We'll refer to the company as "the house."

If you are feeling unchallenged by your current job and you are no longer motivated, or things are consistently not going your way at the company, you can diagnose the problem by revisiting your agenda. The first step is to analyze "the seat." Review all the things that you wanted to accomplish in that job and ask yourself such questions as: Have I acquired the skills I wanted? Have I had the experiences I hoped to have? Have I been exposed to the types of transactions and projects I planned to? Have I built the kinds of relationships and networks I wanted to create? Or, Have I decided that I am inspired to do something different because of a recent experience or something new I have been exposed to that I think is more exciting to me?

If the answer to any of these questions is "no," then there is still room for you to grow and add to your experiential tool chest, and there may be no need to make a change. If this is the case, "the seat" is not at the root of your problem and now you must turn and take a look at "the house." In analyzing your "house," ask yourself such questions as: Do I still like the company? Do I like the people? Do I have a respected voice? Do I like the platform that I have been given? Do I still like and believe in my career trajectory? Are the leadership values still consistent with my own? If the answer is "yes" to these questions, then "the house" is not at the heart of your desire to move on. The real problem is then easy to diagnose. If the source of your discontent is not the seat, nor the house, then the reason you are not firing on all cylinders and maximizing your performance and success is likely another person.

If you are having difficulty with one or two people, this calls for a solution that does not involve leaving a firm or an industry. There is not a person on the planet that you can't figure out how to get around. Instead of changing seats (jobs) or the house (the company), start to channel your energies into investing in other relationships that will help you work yourself around this person or persons.

Never leave an organization because of one person or let one person confound your efforts to move ahead in a company you would otherwise want to work for.

You may find yourself with a boss who is not a good manager, is not motivating you to produce excellent work or to stretch your capabilities, or he or she may be impeding your ability to move forward in the organization because they do not have the ability or power to move themselves, let alone help you to ascend. This can be frustrating, and if you do not know how to move beyond this person, it's easy to convince yourself that the only way to move ahead in your career is to leave that opportunity.

Wrong conclusion! Instead, you should make sure that you strengthen your relationship with your boss's boss and with people in other departments. Informally, you should start to express your interest in diversifying your experience, taking on more challenging assignments, and growing in your value add to the organization. After you have done this for a period of time (three to four months), if someone has not approached you about a particular opportunity, then you should start to more formally seek out particular roles within the company and align yourself with a boss who has the ability to and/or the interest in helping you to continue to succeed within the organization.

Let's look at a different scenario. If you've asked yourself all of the questions above about the seat, and the answer is "yes," and you feel you have fully exploited every opportunity that exists, then it is indeed time to change "seats" (jobs). Start thinking about how you can leverage the skills and experiences you have acquired and sell your way into another opportunity where those skills and experiences are either prerequisites or will be valued as key success factors.

It is important that you recognize when you have outgrown a seat, because if you don't make a change, you risk becoming complacent, capping out your earning or promotion power, or worse, you'll start performing in a suboptimal way because you no longer have an interest in the job and aren't challenged. This is the perfect recipe for making yourself vulnerable to layoffs. If you find that you are ready to change seats, look first for an opportunity in your current house. That is where you have the most leverage. This way you'll have the opportunity to trade off of the performance currency and reputation you've built to gain access or consideration for other positions. If you can't make an internal move, then you will have to consider a job in a different house in the same industry, assuming you are still interested in staying in the same industry.

Or perhaps after answering the questions above, you'll find that, while there may still be opportunity to learn in the seat, you no longer like the house. This might tell you that you have the right job, but it's likely time to search for new companies, and perhaps even new industries, where the same type of job exists and where you can still acquire the skills and experiences that you want. If your job is functional and can be found in most industries (e.g., technology troubleshooter, customer service representative, human resources manager), you've determined you've learned all you can in your current position, and the house has nothing more for you to pursue, then it may be time for a complete change in the house or the industry.

If, alternatively, you decide a career change is in order, then you should ask yourself questions such as:

- What, if anything, did I enjoy about my old seat?
- What skills did I acquire that I would like to continue to use?
- What were the worst aspects of my old role?

You should use the same analysis we discussed earlier in Chapters 1 and 2, to help you determine what career vertical you would like to pursue. And then consider your portfolio of skills and where you could leverage them as a competitive advantage in a new role.

◀ *Carla's Pearls* ▶

1. The decision to change jobs, companies, or careers is among the most important you will ever make in your career.
2. There are always risks involved with making a change. Identify and inventory the risks and be sure you are being adequately compensated.

3. It is worth making a change if you are offered an opportunity with a steeper career trajectory and forward opportunity.

4. If you are offered a new opportunity and you are responsible for creating change in an organization, you must: a) articulate a clear vision for the change; b) understand and assess the players; c) communicate the "why," "when," and "how"; d) identify and define the milestones; and e) celebrate your team's accomplishments.

5. Whether it's due to layoffs, restructuring of product lines, or poor performance, know when it's time to go. Avoid changing jobs because of another person; look for solutions instead.

CHAPTER 9

Managing Through Change

"Our only security is our ability to change."
—John Lilly

In the previous chapter, we discussed how *you* create change in your career. Now it's time to talk about how to manage change when it happens *to* you. I have met so many early and mid-career professionals who have had difficulty navigating their careers after they were part of a reduction in workforce; their boss changed departments and didn't take them along; or they were faced with new leadership after their company was acquired or part of a merger.

Change is not just an inevitable part of any career, it's an inevitable part of life. But change leads to growth, and growth is good. No person (or organization, for that matter) can survive or maintain a leadership position without change. The days of expecting to get hired into a role and stay in that role for years and years with the same company are long gone. In order to stay relevant and competitive (and employable) in today's work environment, you will have to constantly invest in your skills and experiences. As I mentioned earlier in this book, technology has disrupted many industrial processes and protocols and made many other processes, industries, and technologies obsolete. I don't see anything on the horizon that will alter this phenom-enon. In fact, it's likely the rate of change will get faster, and if you want to maximize your success you will have to be com-fortable with and be willing to change.

When a change to an organization comes as a surprise and it is irrevocable (the company is sold, a new CEO is named, a department or division is shut down), it can be unnerving. You are going about life, you are comfortable, you know what's ex-pected of you and who the players are, and then all of a sudden everything changes.

This doesn't have to be a completely stressful situation. Stop. Take a breath. And move toward adopting a constructive, posi-tive posture, an "everything will work out" attitude. Take inven-tory of your strengths and weaknesses, and think about how your role fit into the organization *before* the change. Now consider how it might be useful after the new CEO, or department man-ager, or other change takes place. Think about how your skills can be used in the organization post-change and how you would make the case for you and/or your role to the new leadership.

What Happens When Your Boss's Role Changes?

Helen walked into her office one morning to a request from her boss, Kenneth, to meet with him as soon as she arrived. When she did, Kenneth told her that due to some organizational changes, Helen would now be reporting to Ned, who until then had also worked for Kenneth at Helen's level.

If you find yourself in a situation where the person you are reporting to changes, there are two things you should do: 1) examine the reasons why your boss's position has changed; 2) take a critical look at the new person in the role, assess what you know about them already, if anything, and determine what you need to learn. Answers to both these questions will affect how you behave and how you conduct yourself.

With respect to your previous boss, if he or she is still with the company, consider the following: Is their new position a demotion, a lateral move, a move consistent with some of the changes that the leadership has articulated in town halls or department meetings, or was it a promotion? Will your boss still be connected to your role in some way? Is there an opportunity for your boss to build a new team in their new role?

If the new role is a demotion for your boss or even a lateral move, then it is unlikely he or she will have the opportunity to build a new team or bring anyone from his or her old team with them. If your boss was moved out of the role and the circumstances around that move were not positive, then you can assume that your boss has lost some of his or her political power. In that case, allow them some time to retreat and recover. During this time, it is not advisable to try to access their power or leverage in the organization, as they are more than likely focused on strategizing about how to operate and maneuver in their new platform.

Let me be absolutely clear, I am in no way suggesting that you abandon your boss or the relationship. Notice I said "retreat and recover," because a really savvy person will figure out a way to restore their influence in the organization after a stumble. You don't want them to think they can't count on you during a rough patch. Rather, I am suggesting that you be supportive in every way possible, while at the same time you consider how your role will or won't change now that you report to someone else.

Does the change present an opportunity for you to expand your responsibilities? Will the department continue to be important in the organization? If you believe that there is an opportunity for you to step up or increase your responsibilities, make that known to the key decision makers. If on the other hand your boss's new role is a promotion, then he or she will probably have the ability to bring over some of his or her old team to join them or build a new team. Especially in the case of a promotion, if your boss has acted as a sponsor to you in your career, you should seriously consider seeking an opportunity to move with them.

As you get more senior in your career, the content of what you do every day is not as important as who you are working for and who is sponsoring you. In fact, I would argue, if your boss is promoted and building a new team, the only reason to stay in your old role is you don't like the content of the potential new position, can't see yourself in that function, or your old boss does not want you on his new team.

If your boss offers you an opportunity to join him or her, it sends several signals to the organization about you. First, it underscores your value to the organization. It shows that your boss thinks highly of your previous contributions and wants to continue working together. Second, it signals, at the very least, a pending promotion for you as you change departments or expand your influence. If your boss's influence has expanded in the new role and he or she is bringing you along, then most likely your influence and platform will also expand.

Your New Boss

Now let's turn our attention to the new leader. If a new leader comes into your organization and is respected in the organization, and he or she has a reputation for growing or expanding businesses, then the expectation is that the department is about to change for the better. If the new boss has a reputation as a change agent, while things might be tough in the short run, the organization expects an improvement in the department and there might be an important role for you to play in the change. If the department was previously plagued by poor or stagnant performance, then the new person might have been given latitude from the top to do whatever he or she thinks is best to turn things around. In other words, they could completely change the team. In that case, it is even more important that you have a constructive, can-do demeanor and present yourself as someone who can help facilitate and expedite change.

Taylor was a midlevel technology professional. She was one of four technology people selected to troubleshoot issues for an assigned department and train employees on new software solutions. After arriving at work one morning, she learned that the company had named a new head of technology. The new chief technology officer felt the organization could improve its efficiency and productivity by decreasing technology staff coverage for each department by 50 percent.

Taylor felt her department excelled in its ability to get the department employees to use technology to enhance their productivity, largely due to the one-on-one coverage she and her fellow technology team members provided to the group. However, she accepted that there could be something in the new leader's vision that might preserve the level of productivity with less staff. She started to think of ways the department might maintain the same level of productivity and service with fewer people, and took the initiative to make an appointment with the new director, where she asked for clarification on his vision for the department and offered her ideas and suggestions. The new chief technology officer kept her on as one of his direct reports.

Remember, whenever someone new takes over, they know that their new team of employees have insecurities about the change. And even if the new leader is confident they are the right person for the job, they often have insecurities of their own. As discussed, the leader is usually under pressure to put points on the board as soon as possible. Feeling insecure in their new position, they are focused on discovering "Who is on my team? Who is going to be essential in helping me quickly show progress? And who is going to be an impediment?"

While it might be tempting to keep your head down, staying too quiet during a time of change is a mistake. The new management won't know whether you are a plus or a minus to his or her efforts. At the same time, if you are too negatively vocal, always challenging any new proposals, or passive-aggressive, executing your assignments but making sure everyone knows you are unhappy about it, then you will find yourself pegged as difficult and not essential to the new leader's plan. You'll most likely be quietly labeled as dispensable should the economic environment or business results decline.

When a new leader is given free rein over how to transform a business or a department, then the rule of thumb is usually to clean house, eliminating all the old team members and bringing his or her own team on board. (Politicians do this all the time, particularly in city and state government.)

When I was starting my career, I didn't understand why a new leader would get rid of people who were doing great jobs in their roles. But now, with experience, I understand the reason. A new leader needs to be assured that everyone who works with them is on their team. When you take a senior-level position, there is enough pressure to prove yourself. You can't afford to spend time worrying about someone sabotaging or confounding your efforts to execute on the new plan. And there is a higher likelihood that challenges would come from someone who is a part of the old leader's team with loyalties to the way things used to be.

When change occurs, striving to position yourself as someone eager to execute on the organization's new objectives is critical. Demonstrate your enthusiasm to the new leadership and help them get to know you. In team meetings or at town halls, step up and ask positive, constructive questions. If you have an opportunity, meet one-on-one with the new boss, and make sure that you include the following elements in your conversation: 1) how long you have been with the organization and how long you have been in your current role; 2) your current responsibilities and how you are leveraging certain skills; 3) questions about the new leader's objectives and what they would like to see happen with the department or division.

Also be prepared to answer such questions as "What would you change about the way we currently operate?" or "What would you be worried about or focus on if you were me?" Most new leaders like to test the team they inherit to see how smart they are and to see how eager they are to be helpful. An easy way to test this is to ask the foregoing questions. You should be prepared with thoughtful, detailed answers to show that you are smart, thinking like an executor, and are willing to share ideas, as a good team player would.

If you find yourself in this situation, while you are spending time with the new leader emphasizing your "can do," "ready for change" attitude, it makes sense to also explore other opportunities both within and outside your company. Even if you put forth your most enthusiastic self, the new leader may still choose to deploy a completely new team and you could find yourself without a job. And it would have nothing do with your capabilities, but rather everything to do with the new leader's predilection to build their own team.

On the other hand, if the new head of the department does not have a superstar reputation in the organization, then the signal being sent is that either the department is not as significant to the organization as it once was; that it will be restructured or absorbed into another department; or that it will be eliminated altogether. The new leader is likely just acting as a placeholder until the restructuring is complete. If any of these scenarios happens to be the case, then you will want to find a new job. Under these circumstances, your career is likely to stall if you stay. If the company is undergoing a reduction in force, then the department is likely to be one of the ones the company has targeted to eliminate employees, and if the old boss was your primary sponsor you are likely to be vulnerable.

Losing a Sponsor: What Happens if Your Sponsor Leaves the Company?

A sponsor is one of the most important relationships you can have in your career. This is the person who carries your paper into the room and who, behind closed doors, will use their political and social capital to make sure that you get promoted, get paid well, and get access to opportunities that will allow you to ascend in the organization.

Perhaps your sponsor has gotten a better opportunity at another company, lost a political battle in your company and feels it's best to leave, decides to retire, or even got laid off. No matter what the reason for their departure, the result is the same: you are left with no one to help support you at the company. If your sponsor leaves, all is not lost, but you must move quickly to find another one. In a perfect world, you would have at least two to three sponsors, so that in the event that one does leave, you have someone else continuing to advocate on your behalf behind closed doors.

If that is not the case, the easiest way to obtain a new sponsor relationship is to leverage your relationship with your old sponsor to gain access to a new one. Just because your sponsor leaves the organization doesn't mean that they don't still have meaningful, impactful relationships within the company. Ask them for help and approach the conversation in this way:

"Jim, you have been a terrific sponsor for me all of these

years and now you are leaving the organization. You know that it is important to anyone's success in this company to have someone willing to spend capital on you behind closed doors. I would like to get your thoughts on who you think might be interested and able to play that role for me. Would you introduce the idea to that person and I will continue to build upon the relationship from there?"

If Jim is willing to make an introduction for you, then you will be able to have a frank conversation with the new person about the kind of relationship that you would like to build. The target profile of a potential new sponsor is someone who 1) has exposure to your work; 2) is a decision maker and has the influence to get things done; and 3) has a strong relationship with your former sponsor.

What if the Change Is Losing Your Job?

In tough economic times, companies will seek to eliminate people who have been evaluated as performing in the bottom 10–15 percent of the employee pool. Or an organization might shut down an entire division and choose to eliminate everyone within, no matter what their performance level.

If your job is eliminated because the company is no longer pursuing a certain line of business, then you will more than likely get a severance package based on your seniority, years of service, and other considerations. If this is your situation, it will be easy for you to explain to prospective new employers. You are without a job because the company chose to exit a business. There are no implications about your performance.

If on the other hand the company closed an area, and it is widely known that many affected employees were reassigned to other parts of the company but you were not, you'll have to be more strategic about how you deliver this message to prospective employers. When delivering the message, you should focus on what you gained from the last experience and that you are looking to deploy those skills in a new and challenging way. Do not spend time focusing on the fact that you were not chosen to stay with the company. Your script goes something like this:

"My company decided to close the _____ area and many of us were affected in that decision. Some people were redeployed into new roles and some of us were not. I was not privy to those decisions so I cannot comment on how those decisions were made. I am looking for an opportunity to leverage that experience and continue to add to my experiential skill set, and I am interested in a role with your company because it offers such an opportunity."

Update your résumé, take an inventory of your skills, and decide how you want to deploy those skills and experiences, as well as what you want to learn in a new opportunity. Don't rush to take the first offer you get. You could find yourself being laid off again because the job is not a good fit for you. Or you might negotiate poorly around compensation. Both scenarios could impair your confidence and affect your ability to successfully interview for the next position.

Jerry's company decided to restructure its engineering department, reducing the staff by 80 percent. The company, a parts manufacturer, had made significant investments in technology over the preceding three years, and as a result no longer needed the same level of staffing. Jerry was among the mid- and senior-level engineers asked to leave, while a dozen other engineers were asked to stay on and were redeployed to other departments. Jerry's first reaction was to apply to every one of his company's competitors, thinking he needed to focus on getting the same type of job, instead of thoughtfully choosing other companies or industries that might offer him an opportunity to leverage his portfolio of skills and experiences. He thought that he would be most attractive to an employer that valued the same type of problem-solving, analytical, and managerial skills that he acquired in his old role. Sure enough, he received and accepted an offer from a competitor firm. Over the next twelve months, the new firm started making the same technology investments that his old firm did, and eighteen months later Jerry was restructured out of a job again.

If Jerry had taken the time to think about other industries that might value his portfolio of skills and repositioned himself, he might have found an opportunity that would've given him the chance to change his career trajectory. Thoroughly thinking through his options might have led him to the realization that a competitor with the same strategic vision as his old firm might eventually make the same decisions or potentially even go out of business.

When change like this happens to you, it's important to stop, evaluate, and ask the following questions:

- Is this an opportunity for me to change my career trajectory?
- What, if anything, could I have done to change the outcome?
- Did I do a job that leveraged my strengths?
- Did I showcase my performance?
- Did I have the right sponsor relationship?
- Do I still like this industry and the role?
- What can I offer to a competitor firm?
- What is happening on the competitive landscape?
- Is the industry consolidating? Who are the most likely acquirers? Who are the companies that are most vulnerable to being purchased?

If you determine that there were things you could have done that would have made you less vulnerable to layoffs or being let go, then take stock of those things and remember not to repeat them in your next opportunity. If you determine that there was nothing you could have done differently, then make sure that you have a compelling story about what you gained from that experience and move on to *sell*, not tell, your story to the next employer.

Selling Your Story

If you are laid off and interviewing for a new job, getting the position is especially dependent upon how you sell your story. There are millions of people who have had the experience of being displaced or moved around within a company, particularly during the financial crisis of 2008–2013. You should never think you are at a disadvantage in an interview because of this. Prospective employers understand there are many reasons beyond a person's performance and capability that might cause him or her to be laid off from a company—but it *is* up to you to do the rest.

If, for example, you formerly worked for a start-up, it could be that the start-up ran out of cash or had a failed private placement, and as a result could not keep people on in a full-time capacity. Leadership changes are also good reasons why you might get laid off. You may be identified with the old regime and the new leadership wants to bring in their own team, as we discussed previously. Or, it could be the case that the company failed to invest in its growth and is now under competitive pressure to meet earnings forecasts, and the only way to do that is to cut costs and people.

Getting laid off won't be what will hinder you from getting a new job; more likely it will be your failure to message the event properly. It's a common mistake made by people who have been downsized or fired. They are pounding the pavement, looking for a new opportunity, but they are preoccupied with the fact that things did not end well at their last job. Remember: FEAR HAS NO PLACE IN YOUR SUCCESS EQUATION! Approach anything in your life from a position of fear and you will always underpenetrate that opportunity. Most interviewers will ask "What happened in your last job? What made you decide to leave?" Whether you were laid off, quit, or outright fired, the script for your answer is: "I had a very constructive and productive time in my role at _____. I learned a lot and feel the three most important skills I developed were: _____, _____, and _____. Last year, the company decided to make a change in its strategic direction (or decided to significantly reduce expenses) which led to a restructuring in my department and many of us were displaced as a result (or if you were fired, this sentence could read, "Last year, the company decided to make a few changes and I was affected"). I believe that my experience there, however, has given me the ability to be value add in a role such as this in the following ways . . ."

The key to success is in your response. Answer the question directly, but also take the time to highlight the skills that you acquired from the experience and sell yourself again—let the interviewer know why you think that you are the best candidate for the new role.

A New Role at the Same Company

At times, companies will make the decision to eliminate positions, but may want to retain some of the most valuable talent. If your company informs you that your role is being eliminated, but that it would like to offer you the opportunity to look for other roles within the organization, there are steps that you should take.

First, take a couple of days and conduct a full inventory of all of your skills, experiences, and networks. This way you'll have an understanding of all the things you can offer in a new role and how you might sell that in an interview. Second, while you're putting together this list, consider the "dream job" you'd like within the company. Start there and work your way back to opportunities that would allow you to develop the content needed to make you attractive for that dream job, if not today, then one day in the future. Last, find out what roles are currently open so you can understand the available opportunities.

Perhaps you've just been laid off from your technology support role at an advertising firm, but your dream is to be an account executive there. You might want to consider the open position on the marketing team doing customer phone surveys. In the short term, this could lead you to a job on the focus group team, which would open an opportunity to work on the marketing team for a specific product, which would lead to copywriting, and then to a junior role on a client team, which could lead you to a sales role, and eventually to a client-facing role where you have responsibility for an account.

If you are more senior in your career, then you might want to think about ways that you can value add by managing a department or taking on responsibility for a new product or a new market. Your seniority means that you have seen a lot of things in your career, and that you have a perspective about how to implement new strategies or manage new teams. Extensive experience is something that a younger professional cannot offer an employer, and might provide you with leverage in an interview. You should also leverage your knowledge of the organization and your extensive relationships as a selling point. Think about ways that you can help the company make money or cut expenses to positively impact the company's profitability.

Using the change as an opportunity to consider what you want to do in the future, you could position yourself to move into a new vertical and eventually land your dream job. Once you have thought through all the roles that are attractive to you, begin to network with people who already work in those areas to express your interest. Or if your firm prefers, work with your human resources partner to set up interviews. Your approach to the discussions should be the same as if you were interviewing for a position outside the company. Sell yourself. The only difference here is that you will want to emphasize the points of connectivity you have within the firm.

If it is an area where you have had no previous exposure, emphasize your ability to learn quickly, your hard work ethic, and so on. Present yourself as a good team member and someone who is solution-oriented. Sell your profile as a "safe pair of hands" (see Chapter 7).

If, on the other hand, your company offers you a specific new role, take the time to figure out if the job is the right one for you. As we've discussed, when people find themselves at the end of the downsizing stick, there is a tendency to panic and jump at the first job they are offered. In this particular instance, you'll likely feel pressured to show your appreciation and loyalty by accepting the job. You can expect that the company, your family and friends, and even you yourself will put a lot of pressure on you to take the new role. You might be inclined to think you're lucky to get this opportunity, since there are others being displaced who aren't receiving these kinds of offers.

Give serious thought to how this new position would fit into your career trajectory. Is it in line with your career goals, your interests in acquiring certain skills and experiences, and your expectations around promotion and compensation? If you are interested in the new job, ask all these questions in the same way that you would if you were being recruited into the position or coming right out of graduate school. Understand the key success factors of the new opportunity and make sure that you feel comfortable that you can successfully execute in the role. Remember, while you have just been laid off, you still represent value to the company, as evidenced by their interest in retaining you. Negotiate for what you need to be successful in the new job.

◄ *Carla's Pearls* ►

1. Change is an inevitable part of any career, and although it can be stressful it can work to your advantage. Take a positive attitude and decide how to approach it based on what skills and experience you have to offer, along with your interests and career plan.
2. If your boss changes, determine the reasons why, and look appraisingly at the new person. Do what you can to support your new leader with a "can do," "ready for change" attitude.
3. A sponsor is the most important relationship in your career; ideally, you should have more than one. If they leave the company, engage them in helping you find a new one.
4. Don't allow yourself to be overwhelmed if you lose your job. Use it as an opportunity to craft and sell your story about your skills and experience and why you make the best candidate for a new job.

CHAPTER 10

Reposition Yourself

"We all have big changes in our lives that are more or less a second chance."
—Harrison Ford

I've never liked the phrase "reinventing yourself." It suggests that you are making or creating a new person, a new individual, distancing yourself from who you are or "the old you." Whether you desire to reenter the workforce after a long hiatus, do something different within your current company, or change careers, to do so effectively you must not distance yourself from who you are, but rather *leverage* what your experience has been and what you have done in the past, using it as a launching pad to move toward something new . . . to *reposition* yourself.

There are three steps to successfully repositioning yourself in your career, the foundation for which we've built thus far in this book: 1) Categorize your experiences, focusing on what you've learned and what skills you've developed; 2) create a clear picture of what kind of role you want and what skills are required to be successful in that role; and 3) construct an argument that connects the dots between what you have done and what you want to do now, identifying why you would be effective in that new role.

Categorize Your Experiences

Whenever you are thinking of moving to a new opportunity, as we've discussed many times in this book, you must take inventory: make a list of all your experiences and the skills you have obtained from a professional perspective. Include all the experiences you have had professionally, personally, and philanthropically. Think about all the skills you have developed at work; perhaps you've learned certain types of analysis or built expertise with particular software programs or applications. For example, if you have been a nurse, you might list knowledge of medicines; excellent crisis management skills; ability to think and act quickly on your feet; strong relationship building; communication, organizational, and management skills; ability to multitask; and triage skills.

While you are making this inventory, you also want to note some of your personal strengths. Continuing with the nurse's example, you might include persuasiveness, endurance, tenacity, and creativity. Once you combine your skills and strengths, you can construct a compelling story about who you are as a professional and what you can offer a prospective employer. If the nurse were interviewing for almost any position, she could describe herself as a "results-oriented professional who has strong organizational, management, and relationship-building skills. I have strong problem-solving skills, I'm tenacious, persuasive, and very creative . . ." And so on.

You might argue that these are words that anyone could use to describe themselves, but the key is how you use them when you are describing *your* context and *your* experience and how it relates to the new role.

You should also include the skills that you have garnered in any philanthropic or volunteer endeavors. They might include: organizational, presentation, conflict resolution, selling, solicitation, marketing, analytical, quantitative, due diligence, proposal and grant writing, listening, relationship development, and management and financial skills. I find that people often overlook the strengths and skills they have acquired from their volunteer activities when they are taking inventory. Remember that knowledge and skills are obtained from almost everything you do, not just your professional endeavors.

For example, I have very strong presentation skills, but I will tell you that my real training and experience in this area came from my involvement at the board level with philanthropic organizations. I had given many presentations to members of the nonprofit boards that I volunteered on long before I gave presentations in my capacity as an investment banker. In fact, I would argue that my experience as a board member of these nonprofits helped me hone my ability to successfully pitch for business as an investment banker. You must remember that *how* you acquired the knowledge and experience that you have is not as important as the fact that you actually have and can demonstrate that knowledge and experience.

As you enumerate your weaknesses, be careful not to generalize. Be specific when thinking of things you'd like to improve that would be of value to a prospective employer. For example, if your impulse is to write down that you need to improve your computer skills, think about what you really mean. Maybe you're adept at word processing programs, but perhaps not at building spreadsheets. Or perhaps you are great with spreadsheets, but not adept at database management or software programs that require you to work with photographs. The exercise of listing your weaknesses will give you an idea of the skills and experiences that you might want or need to acquire to be an attractive candidate for a particular role, so that you can develop a plan to obtain these skills or develop a strategy to market around them when you are selling your story.

Steve had been a stay-at-home dad for several years following an eight-year stint working as a bank teller and a loan officer. While raising his kids, Steve volunteered at their elementary school, was the head of the Parent-Teacher Association, coached a youth soccer team, and headed the Advancing Curriculum Association for the school district. In his role as head of the PTA, Steve led the development of the full year's fund-raising activities, organized opportunities for parent involvement, managed the group's financial affairs, and decided on the allocation of funds to various student priorities. Under his leadership, the school had a record number of parents involved and engaged in activities at the school. In compiling an inventory of Steve's strengths and experiences, what could you say about him? What could he sell in an interview to a prospective employer?

Steve is someone who has experience with financial products, understands how to sell (he sold loan products in his job as a commercial banker, but he also sold ideas and opportunities to parents who had not previously been involved with the elementary school), has strong relationship-building skills, is a good leader, has strong analytical and organizational skills, and has the ability to motivate and manage people (including those who do not report to him). Steve could be competitive in an interview for a job in a sales-oriented environment, particularly retail sales (such as clothes, cars, consumer electronics); a corporate environment with a project management focus; a banking environment; a public service organization or nonprofit focused on children or parents; a company focused on consumer experiences; or even at a children's entertainment network or arts facility, such as a children's museum. The key to doing well in an interview and securing a job offer would depend upon how effectively he connected the dots between all of these experiences and the key success factors of the potential role.

Create a Clear Picture of the
Job You Want

While it is useful to use your network to talk to various people and do the research that we discussed in Chapter 1 to discover careers or jobs that might be interesting to you, it is up to you to be able to articulate the kind of opportunity that you are looking for when you are speaking to prospective employers. You never want to seem like you are undecided or unclear about what kind of job you want. You want to give the impression that you were thoughtful and strategic in developing your goals, and to be able to present a compelling argument about how you decided to pursue a particular position or path, why it makes sense at this point in your career, and why you would be of value to the company in that role.

I have known many people who have made the mistake of having "exploratory" interviews with people who had the power to hire them. While you may in effect be "exploring" the organization, if you are looking for a job, you don't want to create a perception that you are trying to figure things out. You want to make the interviewer believe that you have been thoughtful about the kind of opportunity, even if you can't articulate an exact role. The clearer the picture that you articulate, the easier it will be for the prospective employer to think about where and how you might fit in the organization.

Connecting the Dots

There are very few positions where your prior experience is the primary reason that you obtain a new job. Many job postings list prior experience as a requirement, but it is really a "nice to have" as opposed to a "must have" in most cases. No doubt there are some positions where particular prior experience is a necessity (for example, surgical roles, specialized medical professionals, advanced technical roles, and very senior positions in almost any field), but if you are just starting out in a specific career or you are a mid-career professional, you can usually garner a job opportunity if you can effectively sell your strengths, skills, and experiences as relevant in the new role, and demonstrate that you have a knowledge of what would be valued in that role, as we discussed in Chapter 2. You must sell what the buyer is buying. You have to connect the dots between what you have done and what you will be doing in the new role, so that you can effectively build the case for why your portfolio of skills and experiences is relevant.

Marcus rose through corporate America for ten years. He finally became a vice president at a consumer products company, with responsibility for one of the company's emerging new brands. Marcus was also active in his community: he sat on three nonprofit boards, was a trustee at his church, and was an active mentor at the neighborhood Boys and Girls Club.

As he pondered his career and assessed what he needed to do in order to make it to the next level, he had an honest conversation with himself and decided that he did not want to invest the amount of time and focus necessary to reach that level at his company. He admitted to himself that while he still fundamentally liked the challenge of marketing—of developing an angle, a tag line, packaging, distribution channels—he no longer felt the thrill he once did when it came to consumer products. In fact, he was fatigued by the level of internal corporate politics he had to engage in on a daily basis at his level. But Marcus had to determine what he could do with ten years of marketing experience that would allow him to still use his skills, but not be restricted by a day-to-day corporate environment.

Marcus was sure he wanted a role with a more consultative approach, but with a marketing foundation where he could leverage his training and expertise. He thought about starting his own marketing business, consulting to small and medium-sized companies and nonprofits. But he quickly realized he did not have what it takes to be a successful entrepreneur. He did not have the start-up capital, was not willing to use the substantial savings he had amassed over the last ten years to get started, nor did he want to be tasked with the day-to-day business development demands of an entrepreneur.

While thinking about various alternatives, Marcus accepted an invitation from an executive recruiter to meet over coffee, hoping he would learn about other opportunities in the market. As the conversation progressed, Marcus found himself interviewing the recruiter! He asked questions about executive search, the benefits, challenges, and key success factors for the job. Soon, he realized this was an exciting opportunity for him where he could leverage all of who he was. The recruiter explained that some of the key success factors for his job included the ability to source candidates, understand the real specifications of a particular role in an organization, and successfully market the opportunity to a prospective candidate while simultaneously selling the candidate to the employer. Because Marcus was so successful in marketing products to consumers with whom he didn't directly communicate, he thought he would be particularly effective in the role of a recruiter—selling through direct communication, marketing a person by helping them create a personal brand. In addition, because he was connected to so many people through his nonprofit and community involvement, and he had more than a decade of experience in the marketing industry, Marcus was certain he would have no trouble finding clients and a large pool of potential candidates for positions. These factors were all among the connect-the-dots argument that Marcus presented when successfully interviewing for and repositioning himself from a brand-marketing executive to an executive recruiter.

It is important to note that it's even easier to reposition yourself when the new industry that you are entering requires entry-level training and the company that you are going to work for is investing in your education of the subject matter. One good example might be training to be a financial advisor. Almost every major brokerage firm will require specific financial training and testing before you can become a financial advisor. You do not have to have previous advisor experience in order to be hired for the training program, as the program is designed to teach you the essentials of selling financial products, and will prepare you to take the securities exams that will make you eligible to sell them in accordance with securities regulations. The program will also teach you the basics about effective sales methods and will train you how to approach and win clients. Since firms will train you how to be a financial advisor, most of them are looking for people who are interested in helping clients build wealth, have an aptitude for selling and relationship building, and are highly motivated. These firms will also find you attractive if you have a strong network of relationships that you think you will be able to access as potential clients.

There are several profiles of prospective professionals that financial advisory firms would find appealing, such as: a former sales person in another industry (strong selling skills); a college president (network of relationships with high-net-worth donors); an executive director of a nonprofit organization (a network of donor and other nonprofit relationships and experience in marketing, selling, and asking for the order); a professional athlete (network of other professional athletes, a personal brand that will create access to new relationships); entrepreneur (ability to develop, grow, and manage a business); and accountant (network of relationships, experience in building businesses). Professionals in any of these careers would be able to garner a seat in a financial advisor training program if, during their interview, they could communicate an understanding of what it takes to be successful as an advisor and use the key attributes in each of their experiences as evidence of their ability to succeed in the new role.

How Do You Decide What You Want to Do Next and How Do You Get There?

If you have had a number of years of experience in one role or industry and you are ready to try something else, but you are not sure which direction to pursue, you should contemplate what you liked about those previous experiences. Think of the specific tasks that you executed or skills you deployed that you really enjoyed, while simultaneously doing the strengths and skills inventory that we discussed above. Think about the job that you consider your dream job and consider what it would take for you to be eligible for that. When you are thinking about how to reposition yourself, it is important that you think critically about positions that contain the key success attributes that you have acquired and mastered in previous experiences, so that you can maximize the opportunity to leverage these experiences and sell into a new role.

You can use the template that we discussed in Chapter 1 to arrive at the industry and role that you want to pursue. Once you have crystallized the job, then you are ready to reposition yourself for the role. Miriam had been working in a finance role for twenty-five years at a chemical company. She had enough time at the company that she could retire from the company and receive benefits, but she was in her late forties and decided that she was not ready to retreat from a full-time work experience. She knew that she no longer wanted to work in a finance role, but rather, she wanted to do something where she could expand her marketing and selling skills. However, she had had no previous work experience in that space. Miriam began to network with people to discuss her interest in marketing and quickly realized that professionals who were in traditional marketing roles within consumer products companies had backgrounds in brand management, and that people who were in marketing roles within media or publishing either had experience in marketing before entering into their roles or were just starting out in their careers.

One day, a colleague of hers mentioned that she should speak to the head of investor relations at their company because of a potential opportunity. Miriam did not really understand how she would be attractive for the role of an investor relations professional but agreed to meet. During this conversation, Miriam realized that it was the perfect transition role for her because the key success requirements were to: know the company really well, understand the financial principles that were important to investors, be able to sell a story using numbers, and build relationships. Twenty-five years in a finance role had given Miriam the ability to not only understand numbers, but to be able to explain the significance of the numbers and to tell a story using financial terms. She could clearly build relationships, or she would not have survived in the company for two decades, and she knew her company really well after a quarter-century commitment there. These points were all the major components of Miriam's sale in the interview and she was offered the job.

You have decided on the role that you want, but how do you get to it? The most important thing that you can do is to start spending time with people who are connected to that industry or who have relationships with people in that industry, or more simply put, you need to start networking! You need to tell as many people as possible what you are interested in doing, because you don't know who might know someone in the area that you are interested in and can make the connection for you. If there is a company that you are interested in, go online and look at the company's officers and the list of directors on their board to see if there is anyone that you can ask for coffee or lunch, or someone to whom you can, at a minimum, send a cover letter and a résumé. Talk to your closest friends about your aspirations because perhaps they know someone who can connect you to the company. Think about your graduate school and college professors, as they often have corporate connections. If you do not know a lot about the prospective role, then a third to a half of your conversations should be information-gathering sessions where you are learning as much as possible about the role and its key success factors, and the other two-thirds to a half should be conversations where you are subtly selling yourself and trying to position yourself to garner an interview for the specific role.

If you don't have a graduate degree, one easy way to reposition yourself for another career is to attend graduate school in a subject area that would be attractive to your prospective career vertical, particularly if it is one that has a certain graduate degree requirement. For example, most investment banking professionals have an MBA degree. If you want to become an investment banker, but have never had finance experience and your undergraduate degree was in history or English, for example, then going back to get an MBA would give you the best opportunity to position yourself for this job.

When you make the decision to be a full-time student and you are a part of campus life again, then you will be able to easily reposition yourself, because employers perceive graduate school as a bit of fresh start—a reset, if you will. At that point, prospective employers look at you as a new entrant into the workforce and into their field of expertise, and they are really evaluating you based on your graduate school experience and academic performance, and to a lesser extent the jobs and expertise that you acquired before entering graduate school. There is a lot more tolerance for candidates switching careers and, again, the main thing that you have to focus on is articulating your interest, knowledge of the key success factors, and evidence of your ability to do well in the new role.

Marketing Yourself Following a Long Hiatus

Following the financial crisis, I have spoken to many professionals seeking an opportunity to get back into the workforce after being without a steady job for several years. How do you market this change in status to prospective employers? When you have been out of the workforce for a long time, the most important thing to focus on in an interview is what you did during that time to stay relevant to employers and to maintain your connectivity to the industry in which you are interested.

If you have taken online or graduate school courses, participated in certificate programs, or done part-time consulting work, your résumé and cover letters should communicate these facts. If you have volunteered at nonprofit organizations, you should also highlight that on your résumé, and underscore in your conversations with recruiters the relevant skills that you deployed, such as marketing, finance, selling, and relationship-building skills. It used to be the case that if you had a big chronological gap on your résumé, then you would not be attractive to recruiters. If you did garner an interview, you would be at a disadvantage to other candidates who did not have an interruption in their work experience.

During 2008–2012, however, it was difficult to find new employment, so most employers will understand if you have a chronological interruption in your résumé, particularly over this period of time. Don't look at this as an impediment, but rather focus on how you'll communicate in your interview what you did with that time. The important points that will be attractive to employers are how effectively you used that time and how well you demonstrate that the skills you have are relevant to what is needed in the work environment.

If you have been out of the workforce for a substantial amount of time (eight years or more), then you will also have to demonstrate that you have basic proficiency with or understanding of spreadsheets and word processing software. The most widely used is Microsoft Office. Even if you are not pursuing an administrative position, you will still have to use some type of software in any job. If you are not proficient, your general skills will not be relevant and it might prohibit you from getting a job, even a more senior-level executive position. In addition, you should also exhibit some familiarity with social media. Five years ago, it was "nice to have" knowledge about social media, but today almost every organization has a social media presence, and if you are going to be integral to an organization, you need at least a basic understanding of it and its impact on or connection to that organization's strategy and success.

In addition, if you have been out of the workforce for a number of years, you may have to deploy what I call a "step strategy" as you reenter the workforce. This is an approach of taking on roles that lead back to your original position or to a new position that you are interested in. The first job may be a more administrative role or it could be a role in a completely different functional area, but in the industry and in the company that you are interested in. It may be very difficult to reenter exactly where you left, as the industry has continued to evolve, and newer professionals have entered and are continuing to enter the workforce and are in the dynamic queue of promotions and workforce rotation. After twelve to eighteen months, you should plan to move to a role in the direct line of the one in which you're most interested, or at least one that's tangential to that seat. After another twelve to eighteen months in the new role, you should then seek to use your internal network and your performance currency to move to the role (or one removed from it) that you are really seeking.

Sandy had not worked in a large corporate environment for more than ten years. In her last job, she was senior vice president and chief talent officer responsible for workforce management and productivity. She was also the key architect of her firm's diversity strategy and implementation. When she decided to reenter the workforce, she found a senior position in marketing strategy at a large financial services firm, but knew that she would not be as competitive as other candidates with more recent marketing experience. The company also had a position open in diversity and talent management, which required the candidate to develop and implement a strategy to attract and retain diverse talent. Sandy interviewed for both jobs and was offered the job in diversity. Once she began her tenure at the company, she revisited some of the people that she met when she interviewed for the marketing job and began to build relationships with them and other people in that department. When a position in the marketing department that was lateral to the one that she held in diversity became available, Sandy interviewed. The relationship currency she had developed in the department helped her to land the position. Roughly eighteen months later, Sandy was promoted into a strategy position within marketing, a role that was akin to the one that she interviewed for two years prior.

◀ *Carla's Pearls* ▶

1. Rather than reinventing yourself, seek to reposition yourself by leveraging your experience.

2. Inventory your strengths and weaknesses, categorizing your experiences, both professional and extracurricular and philanthropic, and focus on what you learned and what skills you developed.

3. Create a clear picture of what kind of role you want and what skills are required to be successful in that role.

4. Construct an argument that connects the dots between what you have done and what you want to do now, identifying why you would be effective in that new role.

5. Finding a job after a long hiatus may require a step strategy.

Conclusion: Enjoying Success

"There are no secrets to success. It is the result of preparation, hard work, and learning from failure."
—Colin Powell

How you position yourself is essential to maximizing your success—at the outset of your career, once you are within the organization, in relationships, through challenges and change. These are all strategies to help you win! I hope that this book has given you the tools to guide your career, from deciding what you want to do; when and why to make a change in your career; how to navigate important nuances like managing through change and reading signals; and having a level of self-awareness that allows you to discern the role that you play in a corporate environment. In your decades of work, you'll be fortunate to have several careers over that time. Each of them should have content that not only teaches you valuable skills, but that challenges you and that you enjoy.

Technology will continue to be a disruptor and game changer, and as a result there will be industries, sectors, and careers that do not exist today that will be exciting, challenging, and rewarding to many of you. Therefore, the goal for you is to acquire skills and experiences that will make you an attractive candidate as these new opportunities emerge. You should also be nimble enough in your career objectives and flexible enough in your strategies and plans to take advantage of these opportunities as they present themselves.

I bet you've heard the old saying, "life is a marathon, not a sprint," and the same applies to your career. There will be opportunities that arise in five, seven, and ten years from now that you cannot anticipate and that you may not know today that you will be attracted to. Since you will have the opportunity to have different careers over your professional journey, you should not overtax yourself to make the "perfect" career decision at the outset. If you are fortunate to know exactly what you want to do in your career, that is terrific, then you are ready to get started and you should go for it, aggressively!

However, if you are not sure, then start your career journey with pursuing a choice that interests you and from which you will acquire the presentation, selling, organizational, and analytical skills that we have discussed in this book. After a few years, you can then build upon that experience with a crystallized vision of what you really want to do and are ready for the next module of five years.

If you have already been involved in a career, but are desiring a change, then leverage the skills and experience into a new industry or a new role in the same industry. Even if you have already been working for fifteen or twenty years, you still have an opportunity to have at least two more career changes given the new professional work environment. You have a great advantage in your experience, managerial skills, and ability to manage and tolerate risks—these all are transferable to new opportunities.

You have the intellect, you have the tools, and you have the desire to create the kind of career you want or you would not have taken the time to read this book. Go for it and go for it aggressively! You now have the strategies to win!

ACKNOWLEDGMENTS

It has truly been a privilege and an honor to write this book, and I first want to thank God for giving me the inspiration, intellect, and power to do so. God is good all of the time, and all of the time, God is good!!!! When I wrote *Expect to Win* in 2008, I did not have aspirations to write another book. I wrote that book because I had something to say and I wanted to share the "pearls" with as many people as possible, hoping that they would be as useful to them as they had been and are for me. I cannot tell you how blessed and overwhelmed I have been with the wonderful response to that work. So many people have written me, e-mailed me, or stopped me on the streets, in airports, and on subways to tell me how helpful *Expect to Win* has been to them and how it has positively impacted their careers. What a blessing indeed!

As a result of spending so much time on the road speaking with professionals who are at all stages of their career, I realized that there were a lot of questions that were not covered in *Expect to Win*, questions that people needed help with to develop their careers, get past an obstacle, manage through change, or build relationships. After speaking to a lot of Millennials in particular, I heard a need for a new framework to think about how to build and manage a career in today's environment and that is what inspired this work.

I want to thank my agent, Barbara Lowenstein, who has been pushing me to write another book since a few months after the first one was published. Barbara, I didn't think that I had anything to offer you, yet here it is.

I want to thank my partner in writing, Kellie Tabron, who is the best "policeman" one could have. Kellie, thanks for making sure that I get to the finish line and that the words read as they should. Maybe we have yet another work between us?

I would also like to thank Caroline Sutton, an amazing publisher, editor, and friend. You and I have known each other a long time and I could always feel your belief in me and I thank you for it, all the way back to the days of Quincy House at Harvard.

To the newest member of Team Carla, Christina Rodriguez: Christina, thanks for your frankness, integrity of thought, questions, and clarity. All of it helped to shape the veracity and usefulness of this book.

I want to send a special thank-you to Cal Hunter and his team at Barnes and Noble on Fifth Avenue in New York City. You guys are the best business booksellers an author could ask for! I have so enjoyed collaborating with you on the sale of *Expect to Win*. Your knowledge, market savvy, and client-relationship-building skills are second to none. Cal, your friendship means a lot and I thank you for it.

I thank all of my friends and mentees for your inspiration, support, and motivation. The challenges, questions, and "atta girls" have been the wind beneath my wings and the motivation behind many of the lessons that I have shared in *Strategize to Win*.

I thank my husband, Victor Franklin, for all of your steadfast support. You are the best Number One!!! I appreciate you more than you know.

Last, thanks to all of the people who read *Expect to Win*, who took the time to write me e-mails, tweet me, or who had the courage to ask me questions at my speeches: your thoughts, comments, and questions have directly inspired this book. I hope that you continue to get value from the "pearls" I've shared.